too Stubborn to Die

Library of Congress Cataloging-in-Publication Data

Jaramillo, Cato, 1931–
Too stubborn to die / by Cato Jaramillo with Ann Florence.
p.   cm.
ISBN 1-882723-18-X
1. Jaramillo, Cato, 1931–   . 2. Nordhausen (Germany : Concentration camp)
3. World War, 1939-1945--Personal narratives, Dutch.
4. Prisoners of war--Germany--Biography. 5. Children--Netherlands--Biography.
I. Florence, Ann.   II. Title.
D805.G3J3'7   1995
940.53'18'092--dc20
[B]   95-35913
CIP

10 9 8 7 6 5 4 3 2 1

too Stubborn to Die

A CHILD OF NORDHAUSEN

A TRUE STORY

CATO JARAMILLO

with
Ann Florence

GOLD LEAF PRESS

Many of us have forgotten about the mentally ill, the Gypsies, the Blacks, the non-Jews, and others who perished during the Second World War at the hands of Hitler's butchers. I dedicate my book to all of them, so we shall never forget.

I dedicate this book to the most wonderful family I came to live with when I emmigrated in 1954 from Holland to Canada, Mr. and Mrs. Harold Cox and their daughter Marion Cox, who resides in Orillia, Ontario, Canada.

I dedicate this book also to my daughter Louisa Persico, who was only two years old when her brother passed away. She is the only one who, during that time, helped me in her own ways to deal with that terrible pain. She is the most wonderful daughter a mother could ever have.

Finally, I dedicate this book to my husband, Antonio Jaramillo, who is loving and patient and very dedicated to the most stubborn woman in the world.

ACKNOWLEDGMENTS

About three years ago, I walked into the offices of Gold Leaf Press with my manuscript and asked Curtis Taylor if he would be interested in a true story I had to tell the world. I told him I had contacted other publishers, but so far no one had taken my story, and he would be the last one I was going to try. Only a few days later his partner Stan Zenk called me with the news that they would take my story.

Gold Leaf Press selected a writer, Ann Florence, who could help me tell my story. Ann was able to capture my feelings as we worked closely on the book. I shall be forever grateful to Ann and her husband, Giles for helping me to see my own experiences for what they were, and for Ann's ability to help me tell my story so well.

I would also like to give my thanks to Paul Rawlins and Darla Isackson at Gold Leaf Press for their editing and to Jennifer Utley and Richard Erickson for their work on the book's production and design. My thanks also go out to Georgia Carpenter, Susan Coon, Diane Mower, and Boyd Casselman.

Once the writing was completed, Dr. Noemi Mattis, clinical psychologist and holocaust survivor from Belgium, read and responded to my story. I deeply appreciate her insights.

FOREWORD

In the history of the Nazi concentration camps there is
probably no place of labor that bears the same stigma of
wretchedness as Dora/Nordhausen.

KONNILYN G. FEIG, *HITLER'S DEATH CAMPS*

Cato and I met while we were both employed by an HMO medical facility in Salt Lake City, Utah, in 1988. Cato was a registered nurse and I was a family practice physician. I first noticed Cato when she was speaking with what I assumed to be a German accent. She quickly informed me that it was a Dutch accent and not German.

In further discussions, Cato told me of her experiences—of her arrest as a child in wartime Holland and of her transfer to a concentration camp in Germany. The camp was at Nordhausen. When she told me this, I explained to her that we may have met before.

I was a captain in the Medical Administrative Corps of the Army (now the Medical Service Corps) serving in Germany. My unit was involved in the transportation of wounded in the US First Army Sector, from the battalion aid station to evacuation hospitals. The war in Europe took me from England to Omaha Beach, Normandy, in June 1944. From there we followed the path of the First Army through Paris, Liege, and Aachen, including the Battle of the Bulge. We arrived near Leipzig, Germany in April, 1945.

While there, my unit was involved in the release of some of the prisoners of the Nordhausen camp on the southern fringes of the Harz Mountains. Nordhausen was not one of the infamous termination camps like Auschwitz or Buchenwald. The prisoners were initially able-bodied persons arrested for any infraction and sent there to work. They were systematically worked with less than substantial food until they could no longer function—then they starved to death. After death, or near to it, they were stacked like cord wood in the prison yard.

When my unit arrived at Nordhausen, the gates were open and all the guards had disappeared. In the yard were stacks and stacks of bodies. In the barracks were layers of stick figures with large skulls and sunken eyes. A few were standing, but most were lying on platforms four or five feet levels high with about two feet between levels and allowing about two feet between occupants.

A peculiar odor hung in the air. This was not the odor of dead animals that we noticed in Normandy, nor was it the sickly sweet smell of recently killed, well-fed soldiers. This odor was one of mildew and mold. There was no fat on these bodies to become rancid.

Until I met Cato in Salt Lake City, I had largely forgotten the Nordhausen camp. The occasion was so horrifying and impossible to comprehend that I no longer remembered much about it.

Meeting Cato, a survivor of Nordhausen, revived many of the old memories. Only a person with Cato's vitality could have survived.

BLAINE H. PASSEY, MD
LAS VEGAS, NEVADA
JULY 18, 1995

Cato and Dr. Blaine Passey, who was a member of the medical unit that evacuated prisoners at Nordhausen in April 1945.

INTRODUCTION

The Holocaust survivor "tells the story, out of infinite pain, partly to honor the dead, but also to warn the living—to warn the living that it could happen again and that it must never happen again. Better that one heart be broken a thousand times in the retelling, if it means that a thousand other hearts need not be broken at all."

ROBERT MCAFEE BROWN,
PREFACE TO THE TWENTY-FIFTH ANNIVERSARY EDITION OF
NIGHT, BY ELIE WIESEL

I told my story again this morning. The students stayed at silent attention and didn't want to let me go, even after two hours of talk. As always, there were those few who waited for the crowd to leave and told me through tears of their own suffering. I will have nightmares again tonight. And probably tomorrow night and the next night. The hated faces will appear. I will be a helpless child fighting an enormous, terrifying enemy. The screams will be there. And the flames and the fear. I will wake in a panic to find myself far away from those memories. Safe, I will tell myself. I am safe now.

And yet I am not safe. Hate can still find me. I feel it growing around me on this seemingly calm morning in 1995. Those curious, wide-eyed young people seemed incapable of believing that the cruelty I experienced was possible. They think their world is different from mine. It is not as different as they think.

Why do I speak to them? Why do I want to shatter their idyllic world of football games, dances, and shopping trips? Why do I want them to know of cruelty and suffering that took place halfway around the world and half a century ago? I tell my story for three reasons. First, because I promised Martin that I would never let our story die. My dear friend, Martin, wherever you are, you must know that you are the reason

I am alive today. I don't know who has hurt you, betrayed you, or broken promises to you since we were together. I don't know what you have done with your pain. If you are still living, please know that there is one person who has kept her last promise to you. I will not be silent. You live and will continue to live in the hearts of thousands of young people.

Second, I must show young people what lies down the path called hatred. Follow the path of hatred to the end, and life has no meaning. There is unimaginable and hideous degradation. Many of my young friends are on that path. Some have only taken the first step. They hate people for their social class or clothes or intellectual ability. Some are well along the road. They have joined gangs. They carry weapons, wear emblems of their hate, and band together to destroy other human beings. Where do they think they are going? Do they know what kind of world they are creating? They do not understand the terrible power of evil. Their teachers tell them that people are basically good—that they themselves are good. I want them to believe that, but I also want them to know that people can be evil, unspeakably evil. The choice is theirs. I must make that choice clear, and I must perhaps fill them with the fear of what they could become.

Third, I have a message for those who have been the victims of hatred. I know your pain. I, too, have suffered at the hands of others. My sorrows began long before I arrived in a concentration camp. I was unwanted, ignored, resented, abused, starved, and tortured. But I have not turned that abuse on other innocent children. I know what it feels like to have a temper burning so hot inside me that it made me want to destroy everyone I saw. I have carried with me memories of things unknown to most people, but I have not allowed those memories to poison my life. Horrible memories can be the best teachers we have. They can keep us from ever creating the same memories for another human being. I will never allow myself to forget mine.

My memories are my salvation. They have tamed my soul and kept me from being able to hurt anyone weaker than I. They rise up within me and restrain my hands, soften my voice, and help me see with compassion. Your memories do not have to rule you—they can serve you. They can create in you a heart so kind that you cry out in defense of the helpless and harmless. Your memories of pain do not excuse you from becoming strong and loving human beings.

My young friends, you tell me, sometimes tearfully, that your parents never told you they loved you and so you turned elsewhere for that attention, you joined a gang. You tell me your uncle or your father or your boyfriend abused you and your life is over. You tell me that you have joined a gang to be part of its "family." Gangs tell you they love you, but then they turn on you. Your past is no excuse for giving up on life. You can choose today to work and to love. You can refuse to give in to the voices that try to keep you down. You can be strong. I know you can be.

I will never stop remembering and talking and urging you to fight for a better world. The only fate worse than being a victim of the hatred I have known is to be the one who perpetrates it. I would rather die than become as monstrous as the Nazi guards at Nordhausen were. So would you—I promise.

CHAPTER ONE

Children are like empty vessels: you can fill them with good; you can fill them with evil; you can fill them with hate; and you can fill them with compassion.

ALFONS HECK, FORMER HITLER YOUTH MEMBER

It was a sad day when my mother gave birth to me. I was never allowed to forget that I was an accident. Each morning's light brought no happiness to my house, only another day to be told by my parents that they had no use for me. I don't know why my dear brother Derk told me the story of the day I was born. He never did anything else in his whole life that would hurt me. He was everything to me. But hearing him tell about my first day of life used to fill me with a sadness too deep to understand.

Derk was ten years old when I was born in 1931, in that run-down house on a narrow little street in rainy Amsterdam. He was very serious, with a sad way about him that seemed to go deep into his body and soul. "It was a terrible day for you to be born in this household. Especially you, Cato, because you are a girl," he told me with a look of dread in his blue eyes.

The neighbor lady, Bettie, was the first one to visit that day. Derk hated her. I grew up calling her the Woodpecker, like all the kids did, because she wore a little pair of glasses on the tip of her skinny nose and poked that nose into everybody's business. The walls of her house touched ours, so she was never far enough away. She and my mother would call to each other from their front windows as if they were in the same room. Everyone seemed to dislike the Woodpecker, except my mother.

1

Uncle Cor arrived as the Woodpecker was on her way out. Uncle Cor was hunchbacked from scoliosis and had never married. He came to be my favorite uncle, because he always winked at me and talked kindly. "So, Tina," he said to my mother, who was lying on the couch in our small living room, "What did I get, a nephew or a niece?"

"A niece," she responded with no feeling. He picked me up.

"Hello, little—" His gaze locked on my blackened eyes. "My hell, what did you do to her? Beat her with a crowbar?"

"Shut up, Cor. Those bruises will go away in a little while," my mother moaned and rolled toward the wall. "The midwife said she got smothered in my fat."

"I told you that you should lose some weight," Cor teased.

My mother was bristling now. "Oh, shut up, Cor. If you can't do anything but gripe, then go home."

"I'm sorry, Tina," he chuckled. "Where's Gerard? Has he seen her yet?"

"That skunk is still at the bar. I'll send Derk over to get him." Derk raced the two blocks to the bar to call Pa home. He was back in no time. Derk opened the front door slowly and cautiously peeked into the room. My mother barked at him, "Is your pa coming home?"

"No, Ma," he winced. "He told me he would be home later. But he said to tell you congratulations on the new kid." Derk slipped inside, careful to stay out of Ma's reach.

Turning to leave, Cor glanced at the clothes and dishes strewn around the room and said, "You know, Tina, you should clean up a little. Gerard might stay home more often. Maybe he wouldn't drink so much."

Ma groaned, "Not you too, Cor! Everyone is always telling me how to run my house. Mind your own business."

When Cor left, she yelled, "Derk, come take your sister. I've got to get some sleep."

"When can you get out of bed, Ma?" Derk asked.

She screamed at him, "Do you think it's easy to have a baby? It's easier having your teeth pulled than giving birth, you know."

That was my first day, the way Derk told the story.

Derk was more than a brother to me. He gave me the protection I needed from a father and the care I didn't get from my mother. He told me about the times he changed my diaper, gave me a bottle, and bathed me in the water he heated on the potbellied stove. What a lot of responsibility for a boy of ten. He was a bit of softness in a world of stone. Whenever Ma and Pa had a screaming fight at night, I got so scared I just huddled in the corner, crying for the longest time. Sitting down on the floor by me, Derk would let me curl up in his lap. He held me until I was quiet and told me stories he made up himself. I felt safe cradled in his lap, protected from the threatening voices. His shoulder was just big enough for me to rest my head on.

If Derk was gone, I squeezed into the dollhouse Uncle Cor built for me. It had little windows that could slide open and a tiny stove that could cook real food. I played in it sometimes but also used it as my hiding place. No one ever came looking for me there. Somehow I felt safer inside my dollhouse than in the home my parents provided for me.

Derk's life was bad too. "What use are you?" or "Get out of the way!" Ma would yell at us. Ma and Pa called us awful names. Poor Derk got the worst of it because he was the oldest. Never a hug, never a present, never "I love you" or "Thank you." He would mumble and grumble to himself about how he hated his life. Perhaps he didn't know I was listening. I don't know where he learned to love me the way he did.

My brother Piet was eighteen months older than I, blonde and fair like Derk, but with narrower, tighter features. He didn't care one way or the other about anyone. He never stuck up for me or seemed to care what happened to me. He only cared about his friend Bertus. When Ma and Pa started screaming, he got out of the house fast. Maybe he was the smart one in the family.

Most of the names my folks called me can't be repeated. They told me I was a devil on two legs and taught me every cussword they knew. I was a devil all right. I remember the old man down the street who was

Derk, Cato, and Piet

deaf. I liked to sneak up to him and yell in his earhorn or spit in it and run away. I liked to stick my head under the side of the men's urinals by the canal just to hear the men scream at the sight of my mean little face staring up at them.

I don't believe I ever saw my father completely sober, except on the days during the war when rationing dried up his liquor supply. I remember waking with a start to the banging and scuffling sounds of Pa trying to drag himself upstairs to the bedroom. No sooner would he make it to the top, than he would tumble down all twenty steps and sleep the rest of the night in a heap at the bottom. Still, aside from his drinking, he took care of himself. He was tall with neatly-combed black hair. His carpenter's hands were broad and strong. No matter how drunk he got at night, he always got up in the morning and went to work. His name was Gerard, but I rarely heard my mother call him that.

In the one photograph I saw of Ma when she was a young actress, she was pretty and slender. But in my lifetime, I only saw her fat, with

4

stringy, greasy hair. The few teeth she had were brown, her fingernails dirty. Ma took in sewing for people who lived on our street. Every morning the neighborhood women would gather in our dirty kitchen for little cakes served up with gossip and a cup of coffee. She made me run to the bakery next door for sweet cakes. I hated her spending Pa's money that way. He despised those women. He'd shoo them out whenever he came home at lunchtime, but it didn't do any good. They always came back, like flies to rotting fruit.

Our friends in the bakery were Jews. This didn't matter to anyone— almost everybody in the neighborhood was Jewish except us. The wall of the bakery bounded our small backyard on one side. There the bricks were always warm and the aroma of baking bread filled the air. When Ma sent me running next door for cakes, I felt at home. I loved the tidy rows of cakes and buns, the shining floor and counter. The father of the family who ran the bakery, Isaak, always smiled at me and asked me what I had come for, although he already knew. He was short and round, with black curly hair and beard. As he leaned over to reach into the glass case, I saw the black Jewish yarmulke he wore on his head. He took his time to pack a small box of cakes while I breathed deeply of the smells of life in that spotless little bakery. I spent many afternoons there playing with his children, Hans and Jopie, and envying their home life.

At four, I got to go to kindergarten in one of the tall, red-roofed buildings not far away. Derk washed my face and put a big ribbon in my hair. School was clean and bright and filled with hope. I loved it there and didn't want to go home. The teachers smiled and sang and talked to me. I made new friends.

One day, as little as I was, I tried to clean our house. I had never had any experience with cleaning, but I had seen how nice and clean my friends' homes were. I wanted my home to be like that, and I had already made a vow with myself that when I grew up I would never live in a dirty house like ours. It stunk of urine, cooked fish, rotting garbage, and the reeking cat box. The putrid stench was probably one of the reasons a sign had been nailed to the front of our house: "Condemned by the Amsterdam Board of Health." No one ever checked up on us after the sign was put up, and the sign never came down.

Once, wanting to clean the floor, I put about a half an inch of paste wax on the linoleum. That night, the floor was so slippery that anyone who walked into the hall started to slip-a-slide this way and that. We could have gone ice skating on it. I got yelled at and had to scrape all the wax off with a putty knife. No one understood what I was trying to do. Ma wouldn't take time to teach me how to help her. I thought I must be too stupid to learn or that Ma just didn't want to be with me.

I wanted a house like my Aunt Jane's. She was Ma's sister, but we didn't visit her very often. She was blind yet she always kept a clean house. Whenever visitors left her house, she took her broom and dustpan and swept up their footsteps, even when it wasn't raining.

At times, I felt as blind as she was. I felt blind to love. I couldn't see it, I could only feel after it and look for its traces. Aunt Jane's hands moved softly. She was silent when I whispered to her. Why could she see more than my mother did?

By the time I was seven or eight, Derk had a girlfriend. I was too young to be happy for him; I felt abandoned when he left me to go see her. Ma told him he was too young to have a girl and tried to keep him home, but Annie brought relief and joy into Derk's life. They both belonged to a musical group that marched through the streets of Amsterdam. He played the harmonica and she played the drums. Derk told me that he liked being at Annie's house because her mother made very good food and mended his clothes for him. At our house Derk often had to do the cooking himself, so in no time he preferred Annie's.

Once after a big family fight, Derk asked to go Annie's house. "Annie? Who in the hell is she?" Ma asked. She never seemed to remember anything about our friends.

"You know, Ma," Derk replied. "Annie and I have been friends for a long time."

"Derk," Ma said, "you're too young to be thinking about girls yet. You'll only get yourselves into trouble."

"Ma, please. I like it at her house."

Ma smacked Derk's face with the back of her hand. He winced and cried, "Ma, you didn't have to do that. I didn't do anything." He didn't let her see any tears.

She wagged her finger at him, yelling, "I don't want you to go around telling anyone about your family, you hear!"

In spite of my jealousy, I learned to love Annie, too.

On the rare night when Pa was home, he sat by the kitchen table with his brown opaque bottles lined up in a row underneath it. If Ma was standing in the corner of the kitchen washing dishes and Pa tried to pick a fight, she would start heaving dishes at him. He was pretty good at catching them, even when he was drunk. When he asked for food, she yelled at him to go ask one of his girlfriends to feed him.

Once my father had plans to go to the opera. I think he had some girlfriends there. He bought a brand new suit to wear and hung it in the closet. When the day came for the show, he went to the closet to get his suit, but it was gone.

"Tina," he bellowed at my mother from the top of the stairs, "where has my new suit gone?"

She started to cackle and shook a ticket at him.

"So what's that supposed to mean?" he yelled as he ran down the stairs and tried to snatch the ticket from her.

With another laugh she said, "I used your new suit as collateral on a loan. The loan shark, he's got your stupid suit." She grinned wickedly. "And if you want it, you're going to have to pay to get it back."

"*Godverdomme wijf,*" he screamed. He grabbed for a butcher knife and tried to pin her against the sewing machine.

"No," I yelled frantically. "No, Pa, don't kill my mother. Don't kill my mother." I was sobbing, "Here, Pa," I cried, trying to wedge myself between them though I was only about eight years old. "Let me have that knife." Pa shoved me out of the way.

"This time your mother has gone too far," he spat through gritted teeth.

Ma screeched, "If you want to go to the opera with that whore of yours and not with your wife, you can go in your old clothes." They were yelling and cursing at each other something awful. All of a sudden I saw the knife's blade sticking out of my father's fist. I thought I could get it away from him and save Ma. I yanked on the handle, but as he swung around and smacked me with his other hand, I saw the blood spurt out of the hand with the knife.

"Now see what you've done! You cut me! Get out of here!" he shrieked. His rage turned on me, but he had to grab his hand to stop the bleeding.

I ran for the door and yelled back, "Pa, it was your own fault. Now you have to stop fighting." I ran outside as fast as I could, not knowing where to go. I stopped blocks later, panting, my heart pounding with fear. I wandered the streets until it was dark, and then I snuck back in. I found out later that while I was gone, Pa had to go to the hospital and get stitches in his hand.

He never did make it to the opera.

I will never forget my childhood, as hard as I tried for many years. I tried to forget walking around in rags, with holes in my socks and scuffed up shoes. I tried to forget the house I never wanted to go home to. I tried to forget wanting love I could not have. Yet in an odd sort of way, that childhood prepared me for what was to come later in life. What a strange reason to be thankful to my parents—their callousness toughened me enough to survive the cruelty I would later know.

CHAPTER TWO

If there is anything that we wish to change in the child,
we should first examine it and see whether it is not
something that could better be changed in ourselves.

CARL JUNG

There must have been more tender times than I remember. Was I always sad? Or angry or sneaky or mean? Or playing tricks to get attention? Though life was like a dark and windowless room, was there ever a tiny slip of light beneath the door?

Derk brought me light. He would pull me in our little wagon and walk and walk and walk through the crowded streets of Amsterdam until we found a patch of weeds to have a picnic in. We spread out our old blanket, and Derk lit a fire to throw potatoes into. Then we sat and felt the peace of being together. We ate those black potatoes, skin and all. Nothing in my life had tasted as good. In that patch of weeds was love.

And Mr. Speets brought light to me. He was my grade school teacher and let me pour out my heart to him about what my life was like at home. In Holland at that time, a grade school teacher moved along from grade to grade with the students, so I had Mr. Speets as a teacher from third to fifth grade. He must have known from my dirty clothes and face that I needed his care.

My only other adult friend was my grandmother. The light she brought to me was like a dying candle, barely flickering yet still casting soft shadows. On Saturday afternoons, I walked over the cobblestone bridge and through the park to visit her small, tidy home. I liked to visit her because she hugged me and read me stories and told me I was growing into a pretty girl. I hungered for her words. Her soft white hair was pulled into a bun and she smelled good. She told me often how awful she felt. "Must be old age creeping up on me," she'd say.

"Oh, Oma," I'd say, "You're not getting old."

She laughed and squeezed me. "Everyone's getting older and not a day younger, Cato." One day as we sat together, she said, "I won't be here much longer."

"Oma," I asked. "are you planning to die?"

"Of course not, Cato, no one ever plans on dying. But when you do, then it is God's will." She cradled my hands in hers and talked to me once more about God. My grandmother belonged to the Dutch Reformed Church, and as I stared at her withered hands, she told me as she had so many times how good God was. She told me how we should be good on this earth, because when we die we will be punished for everything we do wrong. As her voice sank to a whisper, I thought, "If God is so good, why doesn't he stop my parents from fighting all the time and from beating us up? Why doesn't he tell my parents to give us a little bit of love?" Once again, I wanted to stay with my grandmother forever and never see my own house again.

I had two friends who were twins, Henny and Jenny. They were my age, and like me, they had blonde hair and blue eyes. Their father was a barber and we played in his barber chair and pretended to cut each other's hair. There were never fights in Henny and Jenny's house. They didn't want to play at my house but always let me play at theirs.

Henny and Jenny led me to Sonja, who brought more than a bit of light to me. She shines as a happy memory, for she needed me. I met her one day when the twins asked me if I'd seen the new girl who had moved into the house around the corner.

"No," I answered. New children rarely moved in. "Who is she?"

"Her name is Sonja," one of them replied. "But she can't walk; she's in a wheelchair."

"In a wheelchair? What for?" Always curious, I wanted to know everything about her. I had never known anyone in a wheelchair.

"We heard Ma talking to Pa about it the other day," whispered Henny, huddling us into a circle. "Ma said that when Sonja's mother was pregnant, she didn't want to have the baby so she tried to get rid of her."

"That sounds like my folks," I said. "We should get along great. Let's go see her." I suddenly wanted to meet this girl who might share my secrets.

Jenny hesitated, "But she's in a wheelchair. She can't get around."

"C'mon, we can push her, can't we?" I begged.

"Sure we could push," one of them said.

"Then let's go," I said. Grabbing each of the twins by the hand, I pulled them toward Sonja's house.

As we rounded the corner, we could see a tiny, thin girl sitting alone outside her front door. "Hi," I said cheerfully. "How are you?"

"All right." She seemed a little sad but then opened up. "My name is Sonja, what's yours?"

"I'm Cato, and these are my friends, Henny and Jenny. They're twins. They live down the street from me."

We smiled and she smiled back.

Pointing to her wheelchair I asked, "Can't you walk at all?"

"No. My legs don't work."

"Can I push you?" I asked, staring at her twisted little feet.

"Maybe sometime, but not now," she said. She turned and called through the open door. "Ma, come and meet my new friends."

Her mother's voice came back, "I'm busy right now, Sonja. I'll meet them another time."

"Hey," I asked her, "Is it true that it's your mother's fault that you are in this chair?" No one had taught me that there are some things better left unasked.

Henny and Jenny tried to silence me, but it was too late. Sonja didn't seem to want to answer me, but then she said shyly, "Yes." She paused. "But I don't want to talk about it."

"Okay," I shrugged. "Have it your way." Restraint was not like me, but I never asked her that question again. I remembered all the questions I didn't want anyone to ask me.

"Would you like some cookies?" Sonja asked us.

"Sure," we answered in unison.

She called through the doorway again, "Ma, do you have a cookie for us?"

Her mother called back in a voice that seemed too nice after what I had just heard, "Yes, dear, I'll be out in a minute." When she came outside with a plate of cookies, I couldn't ask her what I wanted to. I studied her smile and the clean hands holding the plate.

"Ma," said Sonja, pointing to each of us in turn, "Meet my new friends, Henny and Jenny, and this is Cato."

Her mother greeted each of us warmly, "Hello, girls. It's nice of you to come and see Sonja."

"It's nice to make your acquaintance, Ma'am," said Henny with a little nod of her head. Then Sonja's mother slipped back inside.

I looked at Henny in wonderment. "You sure are using big words, Henny."

"I learned them at school the other day. So what?" she glared at me.

"Well, don't get stuck up on us." I told her.

Turning back to Sonja, I reached to touch her legs and asked, "Has anyone tried to teach you to walk?"

She shook her head sadly, "I can't even stand on my feet, Cato."

"Well, I'm going to teach you how to walk," I said with determination. I was ready to start that minute. I started pulling on Sonja's hands as the twins cheered, "Yes, we'll help teach you to walk!" Sonja pulled back in her chair, fear etching her face.

"Please, don't. I have to go in now."

"Oh, okay," I sighed. "I better get home anyway, or Ma is goin' to be madder than hell at me for being late."

"Cato," Sonja asked with surprise, "Do you always swear like that?"

"Oh," I bragged, "That ain't nothin'. You should hear it when my Ma and Pa start fighting. You'd think the roof was coming down."

"Yeah," Jenny said matter of factly. "Her pa's a drunk."

Sonja looked thoughtful and said simply, "Oh. Well, I've got to go now."

What would I know of life in a wheelchair? And what could Sonja understand of my crippled family? But at last I had met someone who seemed worse off than I. We would become friends, Sonja and I, and the memory of the few halting steps we took together would come back to me at times when I didn't know if I could take another step on my own.

CHAPTER THREE

*The heaviest wheel rolls across our foreheads to bury itself
deep somewhere inside our memories.*

MIF, A CHILD IN A CONCENTRATION CAMP.
FATE UNKNOWN.

My parents never gave me a birthday present. Uncle Cor built me the dollhouse, and once my Aunt Jane gave me three bright rubber balls. I played and played with them and sobbed mournfully the day one was popped by a car. Other than these, the first birthday present I remember came just before I turned eight. One of the ladies who came over to gossip with my mother was my friend, too. One day she brought me a brand new bathing suit and told me it was for my birthday coming up.

"Now, Cato," she warned me, "I don't want you to swim in those canals, because they're full of rats, and you know that one of them could come up and bite you."

Hugging the suit close to my body, I said, "Oh, don't worry about it. I can swim faster than the rats can. And whenever I see one of them getting close to me, I'm going to dive under the water and stay there until it's gone." I had outsmarted worse things than rats in my life!

Green slime floated on top of the canals because of the garbage thrown into them. The men of the town used urinals on the side of the canal that drained straight into the water. None of that stopped me. I pulled on my new suit, jumped into a skirt, and hurried outside to find someone to show off to. I found Henny and Jenny and announced with glee, "Look at my new bathing suit I got from mother's friend. Isn't it pretty?" I twirled around.

They were surprised because I was usually the one admiring their new things.

"Hey, want to go swimming with me?" I asked.

"Where?"

"In the canal, I don't have any money for the swimming pool. C'mon!"

"Oh, no," Jenny recoiled with a grimace, "Our parents won't allow it." Neither did my parents, but I didn't care. I didn't plan on asking for permission. Then Henny and Jenny started in on the stories about the rats and their sharp teeth.

"Okay, if you don't want to come, don't, but I want to try out my new bathing suit and I'm going in the canal. If I see a big juicy rat, I'll just dive under the water and swim away from it. I can stay underwater longer than a rat. And I'm going to leave my new suit on until Pa gets home tonight," I chattered as we walked toward the canal.

Knowing what Pa was like, Jenny said, "He'll be too drunk to see it. Wait until he's sober."

Henny asked, "Do your ma and pa still yell at each other all the time?"

I had told everyone the truth about home. "Oh, sure! I wish I didn't have to live with them. I hate it at my house."

"Why don't they get a divorce if they don't like each other?" one of the twins asked. "Then maybe your pa could marry someone else and you wouldn't have to live there anymore."

"They would just throw me into an orphanage and that would be awful," I said. "I don't want to talk about them anymore. Come over and watch me swim."

Henny and Jenny stood on the edge while I held my nose and jumped into the cold water. It wasn't deep, but I couldn't see the bottom through the filth. The slippery muck under my feet felt good as it squished between my toes. I splashed around and shouted. It was one of the few times I felt truly happy.

I knew that what the twins said was true. Pa would be too drunk to notice my new suit, but I was stubborn and wanted to stay up to show him no matter how late it got. I was so happy with my swimsuit. I had never gotten anything so new and fancy before.

When I got home, I rinsed the filthy canal water out of my suit and put it back on wet. Then I curled up in the corner of the living room to wait. It got darker and darker, later and later. The cool dampness of my suit kept me alert for awhile, but I just couldn't stay awake. Suddenly I heard the sounds of Pa stumbling, falling against the door, and the rat-like scraping of the metal key against our door as he tried to find the lock. He finally got the door open and stumbled into the house. I knew from his disjointed grumbling that he was very, very drunk. I decided maybe it wouldn't be a good idea to show him my present. I tried to sneak up the stairs to my bed in my parents' room, but he saw me. "Cato, how come you're still up?" His face was slick; his eyes bulged and glared.

"I was just going to bed, Pa," I said. Then he saw what I was wearing.

"What's that you got on, Cato? Well, look at that, isn't that a new bathing suit?"

"Yes, Pa," I said, "but I'll show it to you in the morning when you're sober."

"I'm not that drunk, Cato," he slurred. "Come over and sit on my lap."

"I don't want to sit on your lap," I said.

He lurched toward me. His hot rancid breath made me turn away as he grabbed my wrist and yanked me against his chest.

"Now let me see that pretty suit," he mumbled. "Where did you get that, Cato?"

I could feel his fingers creeping along the edge of my swimming suit straps.

"Pa," I cried, squirming to get away, "Don't do that. I don't like it. Please let me go, Pa. I want to go to bed."

He had me on his lap now, his huge arms locking me in, no matter how hard I fought to get away. "I'm not going to hurt you, Cato. You're my daughter. I just want to take a look at your suit." His hands felt slimy and cold on my skin as he pawed to get them under my suit. I thought of the rats in the canal. "Stop it, Pa." I cried. I started to sob. "I don't like what you're doing."

"What is it that you don't like, Cato?"

"You're putting your fingers inside my bathing suit. That's what I don't like."

"Don't be silly, Cato. I'm your father," he growled. "I can do whatever I want with you." I was terrified of his rising anger. Before I knew it, his hand was all the way into my bathing suit, tugging it off me. I was crying and squirming, fighting to get away. He held me tighter and got very quiet. "You know Cato, your mother and I don't get along at all with each other. She doesn't even like me. But you like your old Pa, don't you?"

"Yes, Pa," I whimpered.

"Cato, you're a big girl now and you know your Pa loves you a lot."

I was crying harder and harder because I knew deep inside of me that he was doing something to me that he shouldn't be. He closed his eyes, as if dreaming of somewhere far away, and I felt his grip loosen. At that instant I jumped up and started to scream, "You keep away from me, you drunken bum." I ran upstairs to the bedroom where my mother was sleeping. My own bed was between her bed and the wall. "Ma, Ma!" I yelled, "Wake up! Wake up!" With her sleepy face, she asked me what was wrong. "It's Pa," I panted as I tried to climb under her blanket. "Pa is trying to do something to me."

"What do you mean, Cato?" She was awake now and annoyed with me.

"Pa told me to sit on his lap and he put his fingers inside my bathing suit. I don't like what he was doing." I tried to snuggle up next to her, but she pushed me away.

"Cato, you're lying. Your Pa wouldn't do anything like that. Get your butt into bed and go to sleep."

"But Ma," I begged. "Aren't you going to talk to him?"

"Cato! Shut up. Get downstairs and tell your Pa you're sorry for thinking what you did ."

"Ma, I don't want to tell him I'm sorry. I hate him." Now I had made both of my parents furious.

She yelled, "I don't want to hear another word about it. Get downstairs and tell your Pa to get his butt up to bed."

"But I'm scared of him," I pleaded. "Don't make me go downstairs."

"Cato!" she screamed, "Get down those stairs. Your father's so drunk he doesn't know what he's doing." She pushed me off her bed and rolled over to go back to sleep.

Like a frightened mouse, I crept quietly down the stairs until I saw my father sitting with his head leaning in his hands, still and sad. Real quick, I told him with my quivering voice that Ma wanted him to get up to bed. I never told him I was sorry. The rest of the night I lay mute and stiff in my bed, barely breathing for fear of waking him. Sleep wouldn't come. Never in my life had my parents told me anything about sex. Not a hint. I only felt, as little as I was, that I had better be very careful around my father.

From then on, the sound of his key scraping the door sent me into the corner like a trembling rabbit. After awhile I developed a sixth sense that he was coming and woke up before I heard the sound of the key.

On the way to school the next morning I told Henny and Jenny about my father. Jenny asked, "Why don't you go to the police, Cato? You should tell them that your pa is always drunk and that you're scared of him. If you don't, maybe someday he's going to do something worse."

"What do you mean worse? I asked.

Henny looked stunned. "Haven't your parents ever told you anything about what men and women do in bed?"

"No." I hated to admit I didn't know anything. "What do they do in bed?"

"Well, they make babies when they sleep together." Henny said, stumbling over her words.

I was so frightened. "Do you think I'm going to have a baby?"

"No, stupid," Jenny groaned. "Unless it was more than his hand that got under your suit. Was it?"

I was scared and confused and embarrassed and angry all at once. "I don't want to talk about it. Shut up!"

"Don't get mad at us for telling you about the birds and the bees, Cato. Your folks should have told you about it," one of them said, and the other added, "And you better find another place to sleep than in the same room with your pa."

"C'mon, we're late." I ran ahead of them to school barely able to see where I was going for the tears.

On the way home that afternoon, I told the girls, "I figured out where I can sleep where Pa can't get me."

"Where?"

"Up on the roof above the dormer. Pa would never find me there. I've been up there with my cat Mollie before."

Henny grabbed my arm. "You're crazy, Cato. That roof is so steep, if you ever slipped you'd get killed. That's a three-story drop to the sidewalk. Why don't you just run away?"

"I already thought of that. But where could I go? The cops would be after me real fast and they'd put me in an orphanage."

"That wouldn't be that bad, would it?" Henny asked. "It would be clean and you wouldn't be scared all the time."

I didn't say anything for a long time. Then I blurted out, "I wish that your folks were my folks. They're nice."

"Hey!" said Jenny, "Should we ask Pa if Cato could come and live with us?"

"No," argued Henny. "We don't have enough money. What about Piet? Won't he help you?"

"Huh, Piet?" I shuddered. "Piet's mean to me, too. He doesn't care about anybody. And Derk has a girlfriend and he only cares about her. They only want to be alone." I kissed the air in disgust.

We walked in silence to my house. I stopped at my front door and waited for Henny and Jenny to round the corner. I couldn't go in. I just sat on the front step and felt doom settle around me like cold, blinding fog.

I wanted to be anyplace but home, and I was forever concocting plans for adventure and escape.

"I know what we could do someday," I gleefully announced to Henny and Jenny one afternoon. "There's a ferry over by the dock at Het ij that goes back and forth to Badhoevendorp. Let's pack a lunch and ride on it for a whole day. And we could pretend that one of us is the captain of the boat or that it's an ocean liner going to some faraway country. And we could swim." I stopped to take a breath.

"Are you crazy? asked Henny with a shiver. "Don't you know that water's awful deep and we can't swim that well?"

"Oh," I retorted, "just keep moving your arms and legs and you'll be able to float."

They suddenly trusted me—I'd won them over again, just as I usually did. "Okay," said Henny, "Maybe we could go some Sunday."

"Not this Sunday," I said. "I'm going to church."

"You go to church?!" they snickered. "You've got to be kidding."

"No, I ain't kidding you. Sometimes Ma comes with me to church." Ma was a Lutheran, and we did go to church, sometimes.

They looked at each other in exaggerated shock and burst out laughing. "Your ma goes to church!" one of the twins cried. "Does she cuss when she sits down?"

"Or does the church fall down when she comes in the door?" chortled the other.

I didn't care if they made fun of Ma, but I wanted to explain. "You know why I go to church? I'm staking things out."

"What are you going to do, Cato? Rob the collection plate?" Henny teased.

"Of course not!" I retorted, wondering why I hadn't thought of that myself. "I'm not going to steal anything. I'm checking to see if I could fix up a place to sleep during the night in case Pa is really drunk, and I can't get up on the roof."

"Cato, they keep the church door locked at night. You can't get in."

"Sure, I know that, but I might be able to fix the door so I can open it up when no one is there."

"What will you do if someone catches you?" Jenny wanted to know.

"I'll worry about that when it happens." I shrugged. "No use losing sleep over it now. I'm losing enough already."

"It's a good thing you can laugh about it, Cato," said the more serious Henny.

"Well, I don't have much to say about it. They're my folks and I'm stuck with them."

"Well," she said, "there should be a law against kids having to live like that."

After a few Sundays at church I figured out how I could fix up the church door so I could get inside. All I needed was a piece of wire through the mail slot. The benches were harder than I expected, but my bed at home may as well have been stone. I felt safer sleeping in the church. One night the caretaker caught me and reluctantly threw me out. "Come back when we have a service," he told me as he scooted me away. How could he understand my desperate need for a haven? Every day the fights at home were more terrifying. Sometimes the police came to break up fights, and Ma was still throwing dishes. Even more frightening was the look Pa gave me whenever our eyes met.

One night I gathered up enough courage to take my pillow and blanket to the rooftop to sleep. My snow-white cat Mollie followed me. I felt safer when she was with me. I knew Henny and Jenny were right—a fall to the sidewalk below would probably kill me. But with Pa in the house and the church off limits, it seemed like my only choice. Our roofs were steeply slanted except for the narrow little section over the window. By climbing up through the attic window, I could pull myself up on the ledge, where I could curl up with my pillow and a blanket. Oh, it was so nice. I felt that I could stretch out my arms and touch one of the twinkling stars. And I couldn't hear my folks fighting at all. Sometimes under those protective stars I thought about Grandmother's God. Did He know I was out on this ledge? Did He care? Could He keep me from falling or catch me if I did?

I watched sure-footed Mollie walk all over the roof and wondered if I could do it too. I knew she had the advantage of four feet, but I thought that with some practice I could be as good as my cat. Sure enough, after I took took my shoes off and tried it a couple of times, I became as sure-footed as she was. Eventually, Mollie and I climbed together from one rooftop to another. I would crawl up one side and slide down the other, stopping myself with my feet in the drainage gutter at the edge. I could even jump onto the flat roof next door, about a meter away. Knowing that what I did was dangerous only added to the fun. I had no sense of my own peril.

One morning I came down and asked my mother right out, "If you and Pa hate each other so much, why did you get married?" I knew better than to stand too close when I asked her this, but she must have been in a good mood, because she didn't slap me. She was never really in a good mood, she was either angry or neutral. But this time she sat down and gestured for me to sit across the table from her. "Well, Cato," she said in a surprisingly soft voice, "you know before your father and I got married, I was an actress."

"You're kidding," I said. "Were you ever in the movies?" I searched her face for a leftover touch of beauty or glamour. I couldn't find any.

"No," she said. "I wasn't that kind of actress. I was only acting on the stage."

"Were you famous?" I asked.

"I wasn't very famous, but I was good enough that they kept me for years."

"Is it scary, Ma, to stand in front of all those people and say your lines?" It felt so good to have her talk to me, I didn't care if she answered my original question. I was afraid that if I changed the subject back to Pa, she would stop talking and shoo me away.

"They teach you all you need to know about standing up and talking in front of people. Anyway, your pa used to come to watch, and after the show was over I got to where I saw a lot of him. We used to go out all the time. He was real nice to me."

"Did you love him then, Ma?" Was that possible? It seemed more unlikely than Ma being young and beautiful.

"Yes, he was younger than I was but it didn't matter to us. Your grandmother didn't want us to get married because he was drinking a little bit at the time. She kept warning me that someday he would drink too much and there would be trouble." She sighed heavily and shook her head. "I didn't want to listen to my mother, but she was right. She had already had the same problem with my father."

I thought for a moment. "What was my grandpa like, Ma?" I asked. No one ever spoke of him. It was as if he had never existed.

Ma responded quickly, her voice rising, her face tightening.

"Cato, your grandfather was a lousy good-for-nothing bum. He used to beat up your grandmother all the time before he died." She looked as though she was about to cry. I wanted to see tears, so I could see that she hurt like I did, but her eyes were dry and narrow.

"What did he die of?" I asked.

"He drank himself to death," she answered, sweeping her hand toward Pa's row of bottles under the kitchen table. As if suddenly shocked by her own words, she grabbed my shoulders and pulled me toward her. "Why are you asking me all these questions?" Her rough voice sounded more wounded than angry.

"I just wanted to know something about my family." I knew I better leave before the yelling started, but she surprised me by letting go and dropping herself limply back down into the kitchen chair. I sat down, too, sensing she would tell me more. Carefully choosing my words, I said, "You still haven't told me anything about how you and Pa got married."

I waited for a slap.

"Well, your father and I went together for a long time, and then I found out I was going to have a baby."

"And that baby was Derk?" I asked with a strange delight in finding this out.

"Of course it was Derk. Who else could it be? That is when your grandmother thought that we should get married so the baby would have a name." I was afraid she would stop if I said anything, so I waited in silence. She went on in a flat voice, "But it was a mistake. We should never have gotten married. Right after we did, your father started to drink more and more." She sat and just stared at the table. Silence. I couldn't stand it. My lips formed the question I had carried with me forever. "Then why didn't you and Pa get a divorce?"

With a touch of sadness smoothing the harsh edges of her voice, she replied, "Because you know, Cato, divorces cost a lot of money. And besides," she went on, reaching to put one hand back on my shoulder, more softly this time, "now we've got you three kids. Kids need both parents."

I don't know why I said it, but I couldn't help it. "But you don't love us, Ma." I knew instantly it was a mistake. She stiffened and her fingers dug into my shoulder.

"Of course we love you kids," the cold familiar voice returned.

I blurted out, "Well, you don't act like it." She gave me a hard smack across the face and I started to cry, not just from the physical sting of the slap but because I knew that this rare moment of having my mother speak to me as another human being was over and could be my last. She jumped up and yelled, "Cato, your smart mouth is going to get you into real trouble one of these days."

I ran for the door and turned toward her in defiance. "Ma, I can see how much you love me, smacking me like that," I yelled bitterly. I flew out the door and ran aimlessly, my tears blurring the familiar landscape. As before, I ended up at the canal and found a bench to sit on until I could safely sneak back into the house after dark. I could never let Ma see my tears or know just how deep the hurt went.

I'm afraid I never thought much about how deep her own hurts might be.

CHAPTER FOUR

War is life.

ADOLF HITLER

As I grew, I spent more and more time away from home and started
playing more with boys than with girls. The boys and I were always
perching in the trees at the park where we liked to swing down and
dangle in front of unsuspecting adults. The girls began to seem like
sissies to me. Ma and Pa must have given me more freedom as I got
older, or if they didn't give it to me, I took it. I still swam in the canals
whenever I wanted to. In the winter the boys and I strapped skates on
over our wooden shoes and skated on the dark ice, jerking each other
around in games of crack the whip. My favorite trick was to get at the
front of the line and pull the chain of skaters right under a bridge where
the ice wasn't solid. When the skaters at the end started sinking into the
frigid water, those of us who had made it safely under the bridge roared
with laughter.

When I found myself alone with nothing to do, I rounded up
Mollie and any stray dogs or cats I could find and went into the hospital business. With sticks and old rags, I tied splints on their legs and tails.
I gave them tender loving care whether they wanted it or not! They hob-
bled along with their tightly wrapped tails dragging in the dirt like broken wings. I would barely get their legs wrapped before they started
chewing the splints off, but it never stopped me from trying again
another day.

For a little while back then, Pa's life seemed to be changing. I
noticed that he wasn't drinking as much, and he was home more often

26

Cato's house in Amsterdam. Ma is at the window.
Below the window is the sign from the Board of Health.

when I came in from the streets. He and Ma weren't screaming at each other so often. He didn't leer at me and grab me and fall down the stairs in a heap at night, so I was sleeping in my bed more often than on the roof.

I asked him one day, "Hey Pa, how come you're not drinking so much anymore?" There were other questions I longed to ask but didn't dare. Questions like "Do you love me, Pa?" "Are things better between you and Ma?" "Am I safe here now?" I must have had a questioning look in my eyes and he must have been in a good mood, because he sat down by me and began to tell me about the depression in Holland. He tried to explain that we couldn't buy as many things with our money as we could before. Nobody could.

"I can't afford to go to the bar so often anymore," he went on. "Even food is getting hard to buy." I thought about what he said for a minute. Then it hit me—he wasn't trying to cut down on his drinking because he loved us, but because he was forced to. I would have preferred a hard slap across the face to the hurt I felt.

"Well, I'm glad, Pa, because all that whiskey isn't good for you," I said halfheartedly. "I know, Cato, but the whiskey helps me forget things that I don't want to remember."

I felt desperate to know what he was trying to forget. Questions screamed inside my head but my throat choked on them. I was very still for a minute or two and then asked only one question in a small voice, "You and Ma aren't happy are you, Pa?"

Pa looked straight at me and I saw for the first time the sadness in his eyes. He slowly shook his head and almost whispered, "No, Cato, we don't get along at all."

There I sat with the man who had filled my life with fear, who had ignored, taunted, and beaten me, the man whose hands frightened me to the bone. At that moment, I wanted to help him. "Well, Pa, maybe now that you're not drinking as much, Ma might not yell at you so often," I suggested with false cheer.

"Ah," he sighed. "Maybe."

"Do you think Ma will clean the house a little better now if you aren't out drinking?" I wondered aloud.

"I doubt it, Cato. I don't think she cares." I think that was the day I began to believe that if Pa had married a different woman, he might have had a better life.

I changed the subject. "How come you've been putting rat traps in the cellar, Pa?"

"Those big brown rats have been coming into houses around the city. They're scavengers—they get into the garbage cans and bring diseases into the house."

"You mean like the plague that people died from a long time ago?" I asked. Mr. Speets had told us about that. I just shivered. Why did a rat in the house seem so much worse than one swimming by in the canal? "Do we have rats in our house, Pa?"

"I don't know for sure. I thought I heard one the other day while I was working downstairs. I'm putting a trap down there and you kids better stay clear of the cellar, you hear?" he said firmly. I didn't like to go into the cellar where Pa's workshop was anyway. It was such a dark place.

About the only thing I can remember our whole family doing together besides fighting was listening to the radio—if there were any stories on and if Pa wasn't drunk and if Ma wasn't out or if they weren't fighting. I mean there were a lot of "ifs" about it. But one night in the middle of a broadcast, Pa suddenly jumped up and said loudly, "Tina, turn off the radio. I have to talk to everyone." We didn't know why he seemed so angry all of a sudden.

"Can't we listen to the end of the story?" Piet asked.

"No, this is more important than any story," he answered gruffly. "There are rumors on the radio and at the bar and on the streets about the German chancellor, Adolf Hitler."

"Hitler, who in the world is he?" Piet asked, already bored.

My father took a big gulp and said, "Hitler is a crazy man. He thinks he can rule the whole world."

"But, Pa," I interrupted, "God is the one who rules the world." I don't know if I believed my own words or only wanted to believe because of my grandmother. It was just something for me to say.

My father didn't bother to answer because he didn't believe in anything. "This Hitler thinks he can get other countries to follow his political beliefs. If he's not careful, he could start a war as bad as the one we had not so many years ago." I had not seen fear like this in my father's eyes.

"Have you ever been in a war, Pa?" I asked.

His eyes grew cold. "Yes, I was in that war, and I saw terrible things I can't even tell you about. I hope we will never have another one, but if this German maniac goes out and tries to rule the world, we might be in for a real bad time. It could even be worse than the last war." It made me tremble to see my father look so scared.

"Why would this war be worse?" I pressed him.

"For one thing, Hitler hates Jews. He's doing cruel things against them to make their lives difficult," he said.

"But why?" I asked, thinking of the air always filled with the aroma of baking bread, of Hans and Jopie, my Jewish friends next door, and their family's kindness to me.

"Why?" Pa shrugged his shoulders. "Because that man is crazy. He thinks that purebred Germans are the best human beings and should rule the world with him. He wants to breed a master race. He calls them Aryans, and they're all supposed to have blonde hair and blue eyes. He says anyone who is one ounce or half an ounce Jewish should be sent away. It sounds like he wants them removed from the earth forever." How could Hitler believe that about Hans and Jopie and their parents?

Suddenly we heard a bone-chilling shriek coming from the cellar. I jumped up and yelled, "What was that?" I dashed toward the cellar door with fearless excitement. Pa got there before me and barred my way—I'd never seen him move so fast.

"I think we've caught our rat," he announced, out of breath but triumphant. "You kids stay up here. That rat could be dangerous if it's still alive." Of course it was still alive; the cellar echoed with its sickening wail. Pa practically leapt down the cellar steps with me right behind him. He turned around and pushed my shoulders down so I would stay put on the middle step. "You stay here, Cato," he insisted. Ma and Piet clung to each other at the top of the stairs. Then Pa's cursing started to drown out the rat's screech. Suddenly Pa was back up the stairs, panting and shouting to me to get out of his way. I straightened up against the wall so he could get by. He bellowed to Ma, "Get me a pail of water. The rat's got its foot caught in the trap and he's madder than hell."

Ma rushed for the pail with Piet racing after her. Pa lumbered back down the stairs as Ma appeared at the door with the bucket heavy in her hands. She was wet and shaking. "I'm not coming down with this bucket, Gerard. What if that rat gets loose? You come up here and get the bucket!" she yelled past me.

Oh, that made Pa even madder. "Woman, bring me that pail, dammit!"

Scrambling to the top stair, I grabbed for the handle of the pail. "Let me do it," I said. "I ain't scared of that thing," I boasted. "I'll bet I see rats bigger than that one when I swim in the canals." Ma set the pail down so hard the water hit me in the face.

"You do what?" she demanded furiously.

"I swim in the canals," I answered right back. Glaring, she wouldn't let me have the pail, so I turned to see if I could help Pa and her hot words struck me in the back.

"I should blister your ass, Cato. I told you to stay out of those canals, and from now on, you don't even get near them, you hear me?" I didn't bother to answer Ma—I knew I could outswim any rat.

I got down the stairs as Pa was trying to choke the rat, squeezing it fiercely just below the jaw. Pa's muscles bulged on his arms. "He sure is a strong one," he said between clenched teeth. "He won't be able to bite anyone when I'm through with him." The enormous rat struggled to get free, its foot-long body writhing back and forth. I knew how strong Pa's hands were—I had been in their grip myself. By this time Piet had lugged the sloshing pail down the stairs, and Pa forced the still quivering rat under the water and held it there. When he pulled the limp, dripping creature from the water, I felt proud of my pa.

"Pa, that thing is bigger than Mollie," I said. "Were you scared?"

"Yes, Cato, and I'm not ashamed to admit it, either." He dropped the rat back into the water and went on, "Come upstairs, I'll bury it in the morning somewhere on my way to work. I don't want it near the house."

I'd had enough for one night. There was a crazy man just across the border in Germany who scared even my father, and a rat had been killed in my cellar right before my eyes. I could feel panic closing in on me. To a kid my age, not even nine years old, the rat seemed like a much more frightening threat than Hitler.

Pa headed for the front door and said, "I'm going out for awhile."

"To the bar?" I asked sadly.

"Yes, Cato. After all this excitement a man needs a good, stiff drink. But don't worry, I'm not going to get loaded."

"Sure," Ma snorted. "You just can't stay away from it, can you?" As he turned just enough to tell her to shut up, she added, "At least we know where we can find you, don't we."

"Leave the kids out of this," he barked, looking ready for a fight.

"Please don't fight," I pleaded. "I hate it when you two fight." Neither one of them heard me. Pa spun around on his heel and left. Ma went upstairs without a word.

"I don't think he's ever going to stay sober, Piet," I sighed.

"I don't think so. Pa just can't do without the booze; his body is too used to it." Much later that night I heard the shuffling sounds of Pa coming home, and for the first time in months, I heard the sound of him tumbling to the bottom of the stairs.

CHAPTER FIVE

I have lots of courage, I always feel so strong and as if I can bear a great deal, I feel so free and so young! I was glad when I first realized it, because I don't think I shall easily bow down before the blows that inevitably come to everyone.

ANNE FRANK

Hitler or no Hitler, trouble followed me like a shadow back then. My life was as unpredictable as that old carnival game where you spot the prize you want and try to pull the right string from a tangled bundle. I kept trying to pull the "fun" string, but instead a disaster fell off the shelf and hit somebody on the head—usually me.

One day the twins and I were walking downtown by the *Kalverstraat,* in the business district of Amsterdam. As usual, there were delivery trucks parked everywhere and on a whim, I said, "Hey, you want to have some fun?"

They had heard that question so many times before, I don't know why they didn't know enough to turn and run the other way. "See that truck over there?" I asked.

"We're not blind, Cato," Henny said.

"Wanna take a ride on it?" I teased.

The girls gave me that look of theirs, half disgust, half desire. Jenny spoke up, "The driver would never let us in his truck."

"I didn't say *in* the truck. I said ride *on* it. See that tarp in the back? If we hide under it while the driver is inside the building, then he'll take us for a ride without even knowing it. C'mon, hurry!"

They followed me, asking questions and telling me why we shouldn't do it. "What if the truck goes too far away? We won't be able to get back home. What if he goes too fast and we fall out? We could fall in the street." We were only halfway there when they had talked themselves out of it and stopped walking toward the truck. Then an even more exciting idea popped into my head.

"I know! After the truck has gone a couple of kilometers, I'll get off."

Henny interrupted, "The truck will be moving. How will you get off?"

"I'll just slide off the truck and run with it while it's moving and then run onto the sidewalk."

"But we'll still be in the truck," Jenny whined.

"Then I'll call the police and tell them that my two best friends are kidnapped. I'll ride in the police car to chase the truck, and we'll all get a ride home in a police car for free." Their eyes narrowed with doubt, then suddenly Jenny's face lit up.

"What the heck, let's try it!" She grabbed Henny's hand and we stepped sneakily toward the truck, tingling with fear and excitement and hoping the driver wouldn't rush out of a building that very second. With Henny and Jenny as lookouts, I sneaked up into the back of the truck and pulled them in after me. We scrambled to get our arms and legs curled up under the tarp and were still panting in each other's faces when we felt the door of the truck cab slam shut and the engine start.

We clung to each other in the thrill of the darkness as the truck began to move. I peeked out from under the tarp. The buildings were passing faster than I expected, and they didn't look familiar anymore. I began to feel a bit dizzy with the bouncing of the truck against my cheek. I hoped the driver would stop, but when he just kept driving, I was scared. "Okay, I'm going to jump off the back now," I announced. I had talked myself into believing my own plan. I would slide off the truck on my stomach and grab onto the back. I would run along with the truck while holding on, then let go and run onto the sidewalk.

"Be careful, Cato. You know you could get hurt."

"Oh, I never get hurt," I reassured them with my usual blind confidence. "And I promise I'll bring the cops after you."

Well, at first everything went according to the plan. I slipped feet first from under the tarp, the cold of the metal penetrating my shirt, and clung to the back of the truck as my feet stumbled to find their stride on the swiftly moving pavement. I was running and running, faster than I had ever run before, and I was afraid to let go of the truck. My legs burned, my hands felt locked onto the truck, and my heart pounded. The sudden shriek of a horn behind me sent my heart into my throat and was the last sound I remember. I woke up inside an ambulance, looking into the blurry faces of two smiling men in white uniforms.

"So you're awake, little one," one of them said to me, softly stroking my arm.

"Where am I?" My voice sounded weak, and when I tried to move the slightest bit I could feel bandages all over me. My knee and head throbbed with pain. "You're on your way home now. You'll be all right."

Then I remembered. "Oh yeah, I was hanging on behind a truck."

At this, they started to chuckle. "Yeah," one of them said. "You were hanging onto a truck all right, but you let go and got yourself hit by a car. Why'd you do a dumb thing like that, kid?" I didn't feel like answering him because my head hurt too much. I reached up to touch my head and felt only gauze.

"You cut your head and you've got some stitches in your lip and in your knee," one of them explained. So I had already been to the hospital and couldn't remember any of it.

"You mean I can't go swimming?" I wanted to know.

The other one answered, "Not for a long time. I think you got more trouble than you bargained for, kid."

"I'm not a kid! I'm a grown up girl," I declared.

"You're a regular little spitfire," one of them laughed.

"Just call me Cato. That's my name." I closed my eyes to try to shut out the pain.

"Uh-oh," I said with a start, trying to sit up but unable to. "What about my friends? Where are Henny and Jenny?" What if they were truly kidnapped?

"They're home, too. The police brought them back. And you bet your life that they're in trouble. I imagine you'll be in big trouble, too, when you get home."

I thought of Pa's fierce eyes and hard hands. "They can get out of trouble, 'cause their folks are nicer than mine," I said wistfully. "At least my folks can't beat the hell out of me this time 'cause I'm already hurt."

The attendants seemed shocked at my language. "You shouldn't use language like that, little Cato." It felt like normal conversation to me.

"Why not? You should hear it when my folks get going. I'm not so bad next to them."

"Yeah," one of them shook his head. "I'll bet."

The ambulance pulled up to my home. I didn't want these men to see where I lived, but it couldn't be helped. They opened the ambulance door, and I could see a bigger crowd of people than I'd ever seen on my street. "Here we are, Cato. Hang on to us," an attendant said.

"Look at all these people," I said in amazement. "Did they come to see me?"

"You sure know how to get a crowd together, kid," one answered.

"I told you I'm not a kid, and my name is Cato."

"Sorry, I forgot. Looks like your mother knows you're here," he said as he pointed toward Ma shoving people aside to get to the ambulance. When she got close to me, she was too shocked to even reach for me. "What happened to my little girl?" she moaned, starting to cry.

One of them explained, "Ma'am, this little girl of yours fell out the back of a truck and got hit by a car." Suddenly Ma was glaring at me through her tears.

"What were you doing in a truck? Cato, if you're in some kind of trouble, I'll tell your father and he'll beat the hell out of you, you hear?" The people stared in silence.

"Ma'am," the one attendant said. "I don't think anyone is going to beat this kid up for awhile because she's hurt enough. She needs to get into bed and stay there for a few weeks. She's got a concussion and has stitches in her head, knee, and lip."

As they carried me up the stairs and into the house, I asked, "How long do I have to stay in bed?"

"At least two weeks."

I couldn't believe my ears. "You mean to tell me I can't go to school or play with my friends?"

"No, you can't, Cato," my mother barked. "You'll do what they say."

If I hadn't hurt badly enough before, now I really felt awful. Two weeks at home in bed! I felt as though my world was coming to an end. But when they laid me in bed, my head hurt, and suddenly I was too tired to worry about it. I went right to sleep. When I woke up, the twins were standing by my bed.

"Hi, Cato. How are you feeling?"

"Okay, I guess." I winced as I tried to shift in my bed.

"Do you know what a dangerous thing you did hanging on the back of that truck? Does your pa know yet?" Henny asked.

"I don't think so."

"Is he going to beat you?" They knew enough to be scared of my pa.

I may have been physically hurt, but my spirit wasn't bruised. "If he does," I answered. "I'm going to kick him."

"You got to start being careful from now on, Cato," Henny pleaded.

"Okay, sure. How about you two? Did you get in trouble with your folks?" I asked.

"Yeah, they told us we can't play after school for a whole month," Jenny said. "And we especially have to stay away from you because you get us into trouble," Henny added.

Years later I remembered this conversation and wondered if this might have been when the twins' folks started hating me. I wondered if this was why they didn't care what happened to me, whether I lived or died.

"A whole month?" I sighed. "It'll pass I guess, but it's going to be worse for me. I have to stay in bed for two weeks."

"That will be awful for you," Henny said, as she ran her finger lightly across the bandage around my leg.

"You think I'm going to stay in bed that long? As soon as Ma is out of the house, I'm getting up and going outside. Just wait and see."

"Cato, you're hopeless," Henny said. I always felt she loved my wild streak more than Jenny did.

I grinned. "You don't think I'm going to stay in this house every day and listen to my folks fight, do you?"

That day, I didn't get out, of course. But the next day I stayed in bed listening for the slamming of the door that meant my mother had gone out shopping. Then I got up. I had a little bit of a headache, but I could live with that. It was such a nice day, I felt like going swimming. So I put on my bathing suit right over the bandages and walked to the canal. I must have been limping, but all I remember was my relief when I saw that water, filthy as it was. I jumped right in and tried to swim. It wasn't long before I became very dizzy. Maybe it was the shock of the cold water on my head or the ordeal I'd been through. I felt disoriented and weak and unable to even stand up. I can't remember what happened next, but someone pulled me out and carried me home. This time my mother was really furious. Twice in two days was too much.

"Cato! What have you done now?" Her rough hands took me from my rescuer. "Listen to me, you get in that bed and you stay there." She half pushed and half carried me up the stairs and put me on my bed. "And when I go out, I will lock the doors *and* the windows," she declared. I just lay there too weak to argue with her this time. I must have been immune to anything floating in the canal by this time, because even without taking a bath or changing my bandages after swimming in that filthy water, none of my wounds got infected.

Ma wasn't finished. After I snuck out, she asked the Woodpecker to come over and sit with me every time she left. I hated the Woodpecker's cackling laugh as she stared at me over her glasses. Why were her teeth like Ma's, so brown and rotten? Over and over again she told me, "You know, Cato, you're going to give your poor mother a heart attack one of these days. She worries about you kids so much. You kids are all the same—you're so ungrateful. Your mother works so hard to make a few pennies because you know your father doesn't give her much."

I just wanted her to go away and leave me alone with Mollie.

"Aunt Bettie," I said, not daring to call her Woodpecker to her face, "Ma doesn't care about me. And when Pa does give her money, she spends it on cake for you and your old biddies."

Woodpecker gasped, "Cato, you got such a smart mouth."

"Well, it's true. Pa tells Ma he won't come home until she's through entertaining you old hags." I had never talked to her like this. I must have been delirious or something. The more upset she got, though, the more she looked like a woodpecker.

"Cato! I'm surprised at you! With everything your mother does for you kids."

The Woodpecker kept harping and yakking and my head was hurting. The only way I could feel better was to tune her out. I lay there thinking about why I didn't like being hurt. Besides having to listen to all the yelling, I couldn't go to school and talk to Mr. Speets about everything that was going on.

After I got better and could go out again, I started to sleep outside under the front steps, wrapped up in a plastic raincoat. Sometimes my father wouldn't let me inside if he was too drunk. I remember him standing with an ax behind the door. I guess they called what he had delirium tremens, or the DTs. When he was drunk he said he could see wild animals flying around and that he had to fight with lions or tigers or whatever animal was coming after him. It was getting so scary to live with him—he became like a wild animal himself to me.

CHAPTER SIX

The broad mass of the people, in the simplicity of their
hearts, more easily fall victim to a big lie than to a small one.

ADOLF HITLER

By this time, my best friend was Greet, a girl I had met at school. Old Greet and I could always put our heads together and come up with tricks to play. We thought of our mischievous schemes together and never knew exactly whose head they came out of first. We were like two firecrackers on a string, exploding so closely together, we couldn't tell where the spark began. You might say we were two of a kind. She was a devil like me. We even looked alike—white-blonde bobbed hair, blue eyes. But Greet was taller with longer legs, so I had to work hard to keep up with her. If we didn't feel like walking somewhere, we hung on the outside of a streetcar so we wouldn't have to pay the conductor. On one of our excursions downtown, we saw a sign on the outside of a Catholic church which read, "Give 15 Minutes to God." After we tip-toed into the dim, candle-lit church and sat down, it didn't take us fifteen minutes to come up with an idea. We watched the people come in and stop by the door to dip their fingers into a small cup. Greet said it was holy water. Each one walked toward the altar, knelt down, and made the sign of the cross by touching their fingers to their foreheads, then to each side of their breast. They seemed to be in some kind of a trance as they kissed their fingers and sat down.

I can't remember whose idea the ink was, but the next day, we crept into the church, and while Greet acted as lookout, I poured out the little bowl of water and refilled it with a bottle of blue ink we had "borrowed" from school. We sneaked quickly to a bench off to the side where we could see everything. Then we huddled up and waited. A little old man with no hair came in first. He dipped his fingers into the bowl and with his eyes closed, touched his forehead and clothes, then kissed his fingers. We could see the dark spots on his head and jacket as he knelt in prayer. Oh, we were dying trying to keep from laughing out loud. Two women about Ma's age came in next. We held our breath, clutching each other, digging our fingernails into each other's arms to keep from bursting out with laughter. We hid there for nearly an hour watching people come and place the blue dots on their breasts and forehead. We ran home laughing and no one ever discovered what we had done. Not getting caught was half the fun.

As Piet and I began hearing more about the German named Hitler, we went to our folks to ask them what all the talk meant. Whenever we mentioned Hitler's name, Pa got angry. "Someday," he told us, "I will probably have to fight in this war that Hitler's starting." Something inside told me he was right. I somehow knew that Hitler was going to start a war and it was going to be a bad one.

"But you can't fight in a war, Pa, you're too old," I argued. There might have been times I said I wanted to kill Pa, but I didn't want anyone else to.

"They don't care how old you are, Cato. They just take you and you have to fight or they'll kill you," he said.

I protested, "But that's not right."

"Well, this Hitler's not right in the head either. He's a lunatic. He thinks he can be king over the whole world. What a laugh!" But my father was not laughing.

"What's a Nazi, Pa?" Piet wanted to know.

"A Nazi, boy, is nothing. He is nothing but the lowest kind of scum. Nazis are mouthless puppets that follow the leader, and in this case, their leader is Hitler and they are killers. Even some Dutch people are becoming Nazis," he said with disgust. "They are traitors to their own country." Pa was all wound up, and it frightened Piet and me to think of him going away to war.

"What will we do if there is a war?" Piet asked.

"We'll just have to do the best we can," Pa answered. "And it might be a good idea to start setting some food aside because things are getting expensive already."

"Then why do you spend so much money to go drinking, Pa?" I pressed him. I was ready to dodge if he tried to slap me.

Before he could answer, Ma spoke. "Your Pa is never going to stop drinking, Cato. It's a sickness."

Pa didn't like being talked about and told us all to shut up.

"It's true, though, Gerard," Ma told him wearily. "You ought to stop drinking."

"Keep your mouth shut, woman," he barked at her. "Instead of always talking back to me, maybe you should keep this place a little cleaner so it would be a pleasure for a man to come home. Why do you think I'd rather be at the bar?" He grabbed his hat off the hatrack and marched toward the door. "I'm going out!" Before he could get to the door, Ma flung her half-filled cup of coffee at his back. The hot liquid splashed everywhere, but he didn't even turn around.

Right then I knew I had to try to fix Pa's drinking problem. And I knew what I would do—I'd heard some kids talking at school about a no-fail remedy for drinking. Before I could try it, though, Pa caught me on the roof.

I was on the dorment with Mollie reading a book when I heard heavy footsteps on the attic stairs. I tried to get over to the other side where I could jump onto my neighbor's roof, but it was too late. Pa's face appeared above the window. "Cato, what are you doing up there? I've told you over and over how dangerous it is. I'm through telling you, now I'm going to show you. You're going to get the beating of your life." I thought furiously for a way to get out of my predicament. The best I could do was to try to postpone the punishment, but then I would have to worry about it the whole time. I didn't get the chance to even try for that. As I swung my legs over the dormer to lower myself through the window, Pa grabbed me and jerked me through the window. The rough tile scraped my legs, and we didn't get downstairs before he hit me so hard I thought he would break my bones. In spite of the countless beatings I had later, I'll never forget the hardness of my own father's huge hands coming down on me over and over again.

I decided then to go back to the church to sleep because I didn't think the caretaker would be expecting me to come back again after such a long time. I was right.

I couldn't tell Greet about Pa's beating without crying no matter how hard I tried not to. She tried to reassure me. "Cato, just think that one day you're going to leave home and you will never have to see your parents again."

"But that won't be for a long, long time. I could run away, but the police would just bring me right back."

Greet was thinking. "You know what I'm going to do, I'm going to ask my folks if you could stay with us."

"I would love to, but I don't think your parents would like me," I told her. I was not likable and I knew it.

"They like you. And they feel sorry that you have to go through all this trouble." Greet squeezed my hand. "Hey, let's go to the market to get what we need to fix your Pa's drinking."

Greet gave me hope—hope that I could get away from home and that we could fix Pa's addiction. My hope felt as fragile as the eggshells Ma tossed into the pile of garbage in the corner of our kitchen, but it was all I had. We ran to the market and smelled our way to the lady selling fish. The lady looked gruff, with hands rougher than fish scales.

"Do you have any eel, ma'am?" I asked.

"Do you have any money, kid?" she snapped right back.

I nodded my head confidently, "How much?"

She picked up a slimy snakelike fish and reached for some newspaper. "Two cents." She wrapped the eel in paper while I dug for the coins in my pocket. As we walked away with our smelly, wiggly, but precious bundle, Greet asked, "Are you sure this won't kill your father?"

"What does it matter?" I said "If the eel doesn't do it, the drinking will."

A few steps later, she asked, "You're sleeping in your own bed again, aren't you?"

"No, I wait until Ma and Pa are both asleep and then I sneak out to the church to sleep on the benches."

"That's awful, Cato," she said.

I felt the sting of fresh tears as I told her bitterly, "I didn't ask for this life."

Greet gave me courage, but I was on my own after I got the eel home. I knew when Pa reached down to his row of gin bottles by his feet, he never looked at what he picked up. He just drank. But I had to wait for just the right time to take a bottle. I hid the eel in the attic and by the end of three days, it stunk worse than the fish market, the canal, and old garbage all put together.

That same day I talked Piet into letting me sleep in the front room where his bed was. I begged and begged him and reminded him of everything Pa had done to me. Finally he relented, "Okay, Cato, you can sleep on the floor. Just don't make a nuisance of yourself." I had a better idea than the floor. I turned a table upside down and fastened a sheet all the way around the legs like a curtain. I figured if I pushed the table up against the door, it would be too hard for Pa to get through the door if he came after me again. That night I felt like I had a room all my own inside the overturned table. Peace covered me in sleep.

A powerful stink hit me when I went back up to the attic the next morning to see how the eel was doing. Ma and Pa were gone so I could finally sneak a bottle of gin into the attic. I had to hold my nose to unwrap the newspaper and gagged when I saw that the eel was changing color and had a layer of whitish slime on it. For an instant, the thought began to rise in my mind that I might hurt Pa, but I beat it down. I carefully removed the cork from the bottle, slipped the beast down inside, then I pushed the cork back in and set the bottle behind an old dusty bookcase. Then I hurried downstairs where I could breathe easy again.

That night the fighting was so bad that I didn't even wait until bedtime to go to the church. When I got there, I pulled the little wire I had run through the mail slot and pushed open the heavy door. Then I sat down on a bench and cried—I felt so alone. As my despair began to crush me, I felt a hand touch me softly on the shoulder and heard a calm voice ask, "Cato, what's wrong?" I nearly jumped out of my skin. I squinted into the darkness and saw that it was the preacher.

"You scared the hell out of me," I said gruffly. I knew better than to swear but I wouldn't admit it. I liked to see it shock people.

"I didn't mean to scare you, little one. I just heard you crying down here and came to see what it was all about." Even in the shadows, I could see the kindness in his face.

"I can't tell you. It wouldn't do any good."

His back straightened. "I don't know about that, a minister can do a lot. But I can't help you unless you tell me what the matter is." He sat down beside me on the bench. "Sometimes it helps to talk to a stranger."

I hesitated, wavering between fear and trust, searching my mind for the words. Cautiously, I ventured, "It's my folks." A sob blocked my throat and I couldn't go on. He waited. Then the floodgates of my feelings opened, and I told him everything. I let the tears and truth pour out, until I felt somehow cleansed. The minister didn't interrupt me once, and when I was finally through, his voice was tender, "I can see you live a very difficult life. Let me think about what you've told me for awhile, and perhaps I can find a way to help." He could have helped by letting me sleep in the church, but he refused. As he walked me toward the door, I asked him, "You won't tell my folks what I told you, will you?"

"No, but come back in a couple of days and see me."

I gave him a listless "Okay."

Before I could get through the door, he held my arm and asked, "Cato, how do you get in here? Do you have a key?"

"No, I don't have a key."

"Then how do you get in here."

I mumbled, "If you don't know, I'm not going to tell you."

"I didn't hear you. What did you say?"

"I'll tell you when I come back," I promised and slipped away. I never told him, of course.

When I got home, I retrieved Pa's bottle from the attic. I pulled the rancid eel out of the bottle and tossed it out on the neighbor's roof, hoping some stray cat would get it. Even if no animal wanted it, I doubted if anyone could trace it back to me. Then I placed the bottle carefully by Pa's kitchen chair.

I stuck close to home the next day. Pa came home right after work for a change and sat down in the kitchen. The first bottle he grabbed was the one I'd treated with the eel. He took a long, long swig. I pictured the snakelike eel slithering down his throat without him noticing and started to laugh. Pa brought the bottle down to his lap with a scowl on his face. "What are you laughing at, Cato?"

"Oh, nothing, just something that happened at school today."

"You're not in trouble again, are you? You'd better not be." He scowled at me, his eyes hazy. What did he care about school?

"No, Pa." He took another swig, dragged his sleeve across his mouth and gave the bottle a funny look. He shuddered. I waited hopefully. From what the kids at school said, he would get so sick, he'd never drink again. He took another swig and almost drooled as he gestured to me, "C'mon over here and keep your Pa company." He couldn't even taste what he was drinking.

"No, I'm going over to Greet's. I'll be back later."

I don't know where I walked that night. I just wandered, unseeing, uncaring. My last hope was crushed, gone forever. Pa would never change. I wanted to beat the kid at school who told me I could cure Pa. He didn't even get sick.

In two days I went back to the church to see if the minister had any solutions for me. He said he wanted to send Piet and me to live on a farm for six months. He told me we could live with another family and learn how to care for animals. "You see, the church has a program for children who have problems at home like you do," he explained kindly. I didn't know of anyone else who had problems like mine, but I sure wanted to meet them if they did. I thought it wouldn't hurt to let him talk to my folks, although I didn't think they would ever let us go.

I told the minister that Pa often came home from work in the middle of the morning for a cup of coffee and to shoo away Ma's friends. He promised to visit and I warned Pa.

"You know how I feel about the church," Pa protested.

"Please, Pa, he wants to talk to you about something for Piet and me," I reassured him.

"Oh, all right" he muttered.

When the minister visited, I quickly put a towel over the chair before he sat down, so he wouldn't get Mollie's hair all over him. He sat down and asked Pa, "Have your children told you anything about why I came?"

If he tells them what I told him, I'm headed for trouble, I thought. But the minister never brought it up. He told Ma and Pa that the church had a program which allowed city children to live in the country for six months to learn about farming. "Are these farmers just looking for cheap labor?" Pa asked suspiciously.

"Oh, no, there will be some work, of course, but the children will also go to school and be cared for very well," the minister explained.

Ma leaned forward and raised her eyebrows skeptically. "How much is all of this going to cost us?"

"It won't cost you a penny," he assured her.

My folks wanted time to think about it, but the minister said a trainload of kids was leaving the next Saturday and it might be our last chance because of the depression. When they hesitated, the minister added, "It's not very far away, and if they get homesick they can come right back." *Me* homesick? I thought. Fat chance.

When they gave permission for us to go, I almost danced over to Greet's house. Her sad face greeted my ecstacy. "What's the matter," I asked. Something terrible must have happened for her to look that bad.

"I've got bad news for you, Cato."

I stopped jumping and started listening.

Squeezing my breath out with a hug, she whimpered, "My folks said they would love to take you in, but they can't because of the depression."

"Oh, is that all," I laughed. "Well, I've got good news!" I told her about the minister and the farm and the animals. Then Greet and I shared a dance together.

Ma threw a crying fit at the train station, but the tears didn't seem real. We hung out of the window waving until we couldn't see her anymore. The minister rode along with all of the kids. They all looked happy enough. Could all their folks be like ours?

Another preacher met us at a school where families had come in horse-drawn buggies to meet us. Piet went off with one family. Then I waited until their neighbors, a Mr. and Mrs. Klein and their daughter Annette, who was about my size, stepped forward to claim me. I liked them right off.

Every day in the darkness of early morning we washed ourselves outside in ice cold pump water. Before school was milking time, and after school we did other chores. I learned my tasks quickly and didn't mind them much. It stunk pretty badly with all the mess around from the animals, but I soon got used to it. The house was clean like I wanted my home to be, and I learned to clean away dirt I couldn't even see. I slept in a *bedstee,* a bed built into the wall, on a mattress filled with fresh straw every week.

School and chores were all right, but I learned to despise Sundays, and so did Piet. It was funny, in the church out in the country, people who were rich had a special place in church with a footstool that could be filled with hot coals so their feet would not get cold. We didn't get one.

Before going inside the church everyone had to remove their *klompen* (wooden shoes) and place them on the doorstep. One Sunday Piet and my friends mixed up the shoes so when people came out they had a heck of a time finding the right shoes. We helped them look for their shoes, all the while laughing inside that they didn't know who pulled the trick on them.

I decided that the minister out there must have been so fat because everyone gave him sweets to eat when he came to visit on Sunday afternoons. When he came to the Kleins' house, we had to sit with our arms folded in a room that was never used during the week and watch him slurp tea and eat all the goodies. After the first time, Annette, Piet, and I decided to stay lost when Mrs. Klein called for us to come in to see the minister. When she gave up calling us, we stole the minister's wooden shoes from the doorstep and sneaked them into the barn, where we scooped up fresh cow manure and stuffed it into the toes of his wooden shoes so he couldn't see it. When we watched his chubby feet squeeze that wet cow manure over the sides of his shoes, we just about split. The smell was terrible! We got whippings, but of course they were nothing like Pa's, and it was worth it.

Mostly it was Ma who wrote us letters, letters that were filled with bad news about Pa's drinking. We didn't miss our parents at all. After a few months, Pa wrote one letter to tell us he was taking some kind of cure to stop his drinking. Piet wasn't convinced. I guess after living with my folks for so long, it was too much to hope for anything good.

It was strange to see the tubby minister walk up to the front door on a day that wasn't Sunday. We thought there must be trouble. He asked me to get Piet which worried me even more. When we came in and sat down, the man told us that with the German armies getting closer and closer every day, we had to be sent home to our parents immediately.

"I don't want to go home," I cried. I had learned to love the Kleins more than I realized. For once in my life I had lived without fear and fighting. I could hardly think of the place they were sending me back to as home. But we had no choice. Hitler could be at our doorsteps before we knew it. He could steal this farm that had been my haven. He could, and soon he would, turn our Holland and my life upside down.

Reluctantly we boarded a train the following Saturday for a quiet ride back toward certain trouble. Ma and Pa greeted us with smiles and hugs at the station. They were so polite, we couldn't believe our ears. I wanted to know about Greet and Sonja and Mollie all at once. I had so many questions at the same time that Ma couldn't answer them all. When we arrived at the house, we were in awe of what we saw. It was so clean. We ran through all the rooms, upstairs and down, into the basement and the backyard. "What happened here? Who did this?" we wanted to know. Ma told us Derk and Annie had helped clean up the place and then Pa gave it a coat of fresh paint. My father didn't have his bottles standing under the table like before, although he did have one small glass of gin at supper.

But the Nazis were on their way, and whatever memories I have of a cleaner house or a short time of peace between my folks are clouded by the stain of war.

CHAPTER SEVEN

*All propaganda has to be popular and has to adapt its
spiritual level to the perception of the least intelligent of
those towards whom it intends to direct itself.*

ADOLF HITLER, *MEIN KAMPF*

I was almost nine years old when Germany invaded Holland in the
spring of 1940. German army trucks filled the streets of Amsterdam.
The soldiers on the trucks stood ready to shoot anyone who got in their
way. It took only five days for the Germans to declare victory over us.
Many times Pa had told us, "Whatever happens, never forget that you
were born a Dutchman. Be proud of your country and never betray it—
we are neutral." Pa warned us about some of the other kids, too. "The
kids you see dressed up in uniforms with swastikas are very dangerous.
They are called Hitler Youth and they are being trained to be killers. Do
not ever follow them. Stay away from them!"

Whenever groups of soldiers or Hitler Youth marched through the
streets, all of us had to raise our right arms and shout "Heil Hitler!" or
take the chance of being beaten.

I was scared of the soldiers, but I was disgusted with the boys in their
brown uniforms and the girls in their prissy blue skirts and white blouses.
Some of them were only five or six years old! I heard these girls called "the
future mothers of the German Reich." Pa said the older girls were told to
have babies for the Reich, whether they were married or not. Some of
them were sent to maternity homes to help produce a "pure" race. Pa said
disgustedly that these girls claimed that they got the strength to give birth
by gazing at a portrait of Hitler. Pa told us he would break our arms and
legs if we ever became Nazis. We believed him.

I could tell by the way the Hitler Youth looked at me, especially the girls, that they thought they were better than I was. I can tell you, no one got away with that. I sneered right back at them. I would have spat on them if I could. I had heard the oath they took when they were sworn in:

I swear to thee Adolph Hitler,
Loyalty and bravery,
I vow to thee and to the superior
Whom thou shalt appoint,
Obedience until death
So help me God.

I was shocked one day to see Henny and Jenny marching by me in the hated uniforms. "Can you believe it, Greet? Look at those traitors!" I said indignantly. The next day at school I noticed how many of the students were wearing the uniforms. Seeing our principal in the uniform of the SS almost made me throw up. When I cornered Henny and Jenny, they told me their father had joined the SS.

"Cato, our father told us that if we joined Hitler Youth, we'd always have enough food to eat. You should join, too," one of them said.

"Pa would kill me if I ever did that," I declared. I didn't talk to them very much after that.

Our small yard that Pa had covered with flat stones from the fields was to play a very important part in our lives during the war. The yard was surrounded by walls on each side. One wall was the bakery's, one was the Woodpecker's, one belonged to us and the other to someone who lived on the street behind us. Slanting up against the bakery was the coal bin where Pa stored fuel for our potbellied stove. Pa said the warmth from the bakery wall helped keep the wood and coal dry. In the tiny courtyard, there was a little patch of soil where Derk once planted flower seeds. A few flowers bloomed, and a little tree even tried to grow, but it never got very big because Mollie would often swing from the branches and break them.

Cato's mother and Mollie. Ma is standing in the backyard.
Cato's family buried cans of food under the stones during the war.
To Ma's right are the windows to the basement
Cato's family used as a bomb shelter.

That small patch of dirt became a graveyard for any of Mollie's kittens that died. I wrapped each kitten in tissue paper and placed it in a shoe box. Then I tied a cross out of two sticks, held a private funeral, and buried them. The flowers always grew better where the cats were buried.

I remember once waiting a couple of weeks and digging one of the kittens up. I had to see what death looked like. Waiting until no one was home, I got down on my hands and knees and dug into the soft soil where I had placed a little cross made of sticks. Carefully opening the damp lid, I recoiled from the smell. I held my breath and studied the stiff little body with fascination. The paws were curled up, the body was sunken and seemed hollow where plumpness had been. I knew I shouldn't, but I had to touch it. The cold fur was still soft. I closed the box and buried it again. Then I took Mollie up into my room and clutched her fat body in my arms for a long, long time. I found comfort in her purring.

I dug the box up and peeked inside every few days until I had satisfied my curiosity.

I can't remember exactly how old I was when Derk began to slowly fade out of my life, but by the time Germany invaded he spent very little time at home. I knew he hated my parents, and I knew he was in love with beautiful Annie. He began spending more and more time with her family. At first he would go out with her after dinner and come back very late. Then he gradually stopped coming home for supper. I didn't blame him—Ma's cooking didn't make anybody want to eat.

He told me that Annie's house was clean and that her parents liked to talk to him. There were many nights I didn't know where he slept. That meant he didn't know where I was sleeping either. I only hoped that he was in a bed and not perched up on someone's roof or in the street. Even though I knew he didn't want to, he still came home once in awhile. I wanted to believe he came to see if I was all right, though it might have been that he was just coming to get something that he needed. But one day Derk did appear in our doorway just when Piet and I desperately needed him.

A week earlier, as I was getting ready for school, I had heard the familiar sound of my mother yelling out of the window for the Woodpecker. "Bettie," she hollered. "Come down for a cup of coffee?"

Before I could escape to school, Bettie was inside the front door, and Ma was saying she had something important to tell her. Being as nosy as I was, I lingered at the door, pretending to be busy with something.

"You know that problem I've been having with my eyes lately?" I heard Ma ask the Woodpecker.

"Yes," the Woodpecker pounced on it instantly. "It's all that sewing you have been doing. I told you that you've been doing too much of it."

"No," Ma replied, "I went to a doctor and he told me I've got cataracts on my eyes and he wants to take them off." For once, the Woodpecker was quiet.

Ma went on, "I need someone to stay with the kids while I'm at the hospital. I got to make sure someone will feed them. Can you do it, Bettie?"

"What about your husband?" the Woodpecker squawked. "Why can't he do it?"

Ma answered sadly, "I know him. He won't stick around even if he says he will."

That old Woodpecker thought about it for a few minutes and then answered, "Well, I suppose I could take care of the kids. But I'm not going to wait around to feed Gerard when he gets home from the bar!"

Ma snorted, "I don't care if he eats or not. Let one of his girlfriends feed him."

It was bad enough that our folks had to fight and this busybody would come running to stick her nose into it, but now she was going to be around every day taking care of Piet and me. As Ma was leaving for the hospital, the Woodpecker asked her, "What about Piet? Does he still pee in the bed?"

"Of course," Ma said. "He hasn't overcome the kidney problem yet. Maybe someday he'll grow out of it."

I didn't want to hear any more. I slipped out of the front door trying to hold in the tears. How many times had I fled down my street, tears blurring the cracks in the sidewalk, the bricks in the road, and the silhouettes of trees. Was it the tears or the anger that left me never quite able to see my world clearly?

With the Woodpecker there so much, Pa spent even more of his time at the bar. The first night, she came over to get Piet out of bed to go to the bathroom, so his bed was dry when he got up. The second night she didn't bother coming, and that morning Piet was smelly and wet. She was furious.

"Piet," she said grimly. "I'm going to teach you a lesson you'll never forget. You're just lazy and there's no reason for you to pee in your bed." She marched outside and filled our mop bucket with freezing cold water. She came back and jerked Piet by the arm, demanding, "Take your pants down, boy and get down there."

I could sense the fear shoot through Piet as he tried to pull away from her. He asked with a shiver, "What are you going to do to me? What's that water for?"

"Stop that whining. You're going to sit in there until you learn that this is what you're going to get every day if you pee in your bed." Tightening her grip, she repeated in a sharper voice, "Now take down your pants." He was no match for her strength. She grabbed his wrists and shoved him into the bucket. Piet just screamed and screamed, splashing cold water on Woodpecker as he struggled to get out. But she held him there, her face and dress dripping. Then he started to kick her.

"You witch," I screamed. Piet was kicking her hard enough to really hurt her, but I didn't care. It was my own brother she had in there. Consumed by a wave of fury, I kicked my wooden clogs into her legs as hard as I could. I kicked her again and again until she had to let him go. Piet and I stood there, shaking and crying. I wanted the Woodpecker to be crying too, but the only water on her face was from the bucket. She seemed too mean to cry. Just then, Derk appeared in our doorway.

"What's going on here? I could hear you two yelling all the way across the city." Then he saw the bucket, Piet's bare bottom, and the Woodpecker standing there all wet with her hands on her hips glaring at him. He didn't wait for an explanation. "Bettie, what are doing to these kids?"

"I'm teaching your brother to keep his bed dry, that's what I'm doing. And if your drunk of a father was ever around I wouldn't even have to be here."

Derk was so mad, he was just about spitting nails. "And you think you can stop him by freezing his hind end off?" he raged. I thought for a moment he was going to hit her. But he only shook his fist just short of her nose and demanded in a voice stronger than I had ever heard Derk use, "Get out of here. I'll take care of these kids while my mother's in the hospital. Don't show your face back here again." He seemed to fill the room with his power.

The Woodpecker looked so self-righteous. Straightening her dress, she pulled her shoulders back to try to regain her dignity. "Well," she sniffed, "and that's the thanks I get." Then she stomped out.

Piet dashed upstairs to escape more embarrassment, and I ran into my brother's arms. "Derk, are you sure she's not going to come back?"

"Not if I can help it, Cato." He hugged me to him. How I had missed his strong arms and reassuring voice. "Now hurry up and get to school or you're going to be late." I knew Derk would be making a sacrifice to stay with us, because he was living permanently with his girlfriend's family since he had gotten a job.

"But what will Annie say when she finds out you're going to be here with us?" I asked him.

"Don't worry, little sister, she's not going to say anything," he said, tickling me lightly under my chin.

I wrapped my arms around his waist, wanting to hold him forever. With Derk here, my upside down world suddenly began to feel steady. "I wish you could live with us here again. Can't you come back? Please?" I begged him. Even as I begged, I knew it wasn't fair to ask Derk to come back. His hollow, tormented look was gone since living with Annie's family. But I needed him so.

"You know that's not possible, Cato. I couldn't get any sleep here with all the fighting, and it was affecting my job." He let me hold on a little longer and then shook me loose, lifted me up, and swung me around. "Besides, Annie and I are going to get married before too long."

"You are?" I asked, trying to smile through the pain that suddenly pierced me. I wanted him to be happy, but how could he leave me behind? "Are you going to have a big wedding?" I managed to ask.

I slipped down from his arms as he laughed. "Not too big. I just hope Ma and Pa won't pick a fight while we're saying our vows. If they do that, I'm going to throw them out."

"I would like to see you do that, Derk, because Pa's awful strong."

"I know that, but he's not going to ruin my wedding."

Piet came back down the stairs properly dressed for school but still shivering. I knew we had to hurry, but I stopped to ask Derk, "Will you be here when we get back from school?"

"I'll be at the office until five o'clock, and you need to give me a few minutes to get home." Something in my face revealed my fears. He asked, "You're not afraid to stay in the house by yourself are you?"

How could he have forgotten what I had told him about Pa and me? "Yes," I whispered. Though Pa almost always went straight to the bar from work, I knew there was a small chance he would stop by home on his way or come home from the bar when I was still awake. I was terrified.

"Why?" he questioned. All at once, the look of knowing came into his eyes and he hugged me again. "The best thing to do is not to be in the same room with Pa when he's drunk. When he's drunk, he doesn't know what he's doing." He took me by both arms, "Cato, promise me you'll be careful. I will be here just as soon as I can. Now go to school."

Piet and I walked to school in silence. The events of the morning wouldn't leave my mind. Mr. Speets let me talk to him while the other children went to recess outside. I didn't feel like playing anyway. As I had so many times before, I told him everything—about the Woodpecker's cruelty, about the fighting I knew would start as soon as Ma came home from the hospital, about Derk's new life with Annie. Mr. Speets looked unhappy and concerned. He was a young man, tall, with black neatly combed hair. His hands were large and strong like my father's, yet their strength had guided me through books instead of lessons in terror. I liked watching his hands as he wrote on the blackboard. I remember, too, how his fingers would tighten into a fist as he listened to me recount my troubles, and wondered if he wanted to hurt Pa. I wanted his strength on my side. I should have known Mr. Speets would never use his hands to inflict pain, even on Pa.

"Cato, tell me the next time one of your parents has to go away. I'll see to it that you and Piet are placed in another home," he told me gently.

"What do you mean? You're not talking about an orphanage are you, Mr. Speets?"

"Do you have something against an orphanage? Have you ever been in one?"

"No, but my friends told me that they're very strict in there, and they beat you if you do something wrong."

"No, Cato, they don't beat you." he reassured me.

I wouldn't think of hugging a teacher, no matter how much I longed to. Why couldn't he take me home with him? As much as I loved him, it hurt to know that someone had a father like Mr. Speets, while I went home every night to someone who seemed to hate me.

Then he changed the subject. "Have you ever been to a museum, Cato?" he asked.

"I've never heard of a museum. What do you do there?"

The other children in my class began rushing in from recess, panting and red-cheeked. I wished recess was longer and that our short time of quiet didn't have to end. "Just a minute, Cato, and I'll explain it to the whole class."

I found my seat and waited for his explanation. Was a museum some kind of orphanage? Was it some place that might punish my parents? Could it be an escape for my brother and me?

As soon as Mr. Speets starting talking, I understood that the museum wasn't a place just for Piet and me, but a place the whole class would be going to visit. The Woodpecker faded from memory as I joined in the excitement. Mr. Speets announced, "All of you kids will have to bring five cents for the streetcar. Have any of you ever been in a streetcar?"

One kid yelled, "I've hung on the outside of one." I knew all about that. I'd been *on* a streetcar hundreds of times, but never *in* one. Mr. Speets brushed his hand toward us, "That's not what I mean. Now look, I want you all to come next Thursday dressed in your best clothes and ready to have fun, okay?"

My excitement was instantly deflated by the thought of my "best clothes." Besides the shabby jumper I wore every day to school, I had only one "best" dress, and it was so old, I was afraid to have anyone see it. I couldn't go anywhere in that faded old rag. I would feel like a beggar among royalty. I could think of a good lie to explain to Ma why I couldn't go to school that day. As we bent our heads over our arithmetic assignment, I glanced up and caught Mr. Speets looking at me with an expression of affection. Because I had never been able to expect it, tenderness always surprised me, much like I felt at the first touch of green after a long, gray winter. Every winter I forgot what green was like, just as I kept forgetting that love existed.

While the other students worked quietly, I walked timidly up to Mr. Speets' desk and took a place in the line of students waiting for his help. I studied my paper and tried to look like it was arithmetic help I needed.

Finally it was my turn. I bent over his desk with my paper in front of him and whispered in his ear, "I can't go to the museum because my dress is too old."

"It will be all right, Cato," he answered quietly, touching my hand. "You just wear whatever you have and don't worry." I walked back to my desk sadly.

All the while my mother was at the hospital, I thought about my old dress. I took it out of the closet, hoping it wasn't as bad as I remembered. It was. It hung limp as an old string, and the color had faded into a dirty gray. After Ma had been home a couple of days and she wasn't moaning so much about her pain, I asked her in my sweetest voice, "Ma, can you make a new dress for me?"

"Whatever for, Cato?" she said. "There isn't anything wrong with your other dress."

I carefully chose my words. "Well, we're going to the museum with Mr. Speets and the other kids. He told us to wear our very best clothes. I like how you made my dress, but don't you think it's getting a little too small for me?" Her silence made me keep trying. "You're always making things for other people, so why can't you make something for me?"

"I make clothes for other people because I get paid for them," she said.

"You mean you want your own kids to pay for them, too?" I asked.

"Oh, go on outside and I'll see what I can do. Maybe I have a piece of material lying around."

I moved closer to give her a hug. "Ma," I said happily, "can I give you a hug?"

But she waved me off. "Go on, Cato." Her words made me feel sad again. But that night when I came in, my mother surprised me with a new dress. It was very simply made of blue and white cotton, but to me it was the most beautiful dress in the world. As I left for school the next day I told her for the first time in my life that I loved her. I don't know if she even heard me.

CHAPTER EIGHT

There are worse things waiting for men than death.

A.C. SWINBURNE, *THE TRIUMPH OF TIME*

I was so excited about the dress that I wrapped it in newspaper to keep it from getting dirty and took it to school to show Mr. Speets. Again I waited for the others to go outside and then unwrapped the paper to show him my surprise. He looked very happy and said, "Cato, it is a very pretty dress, and it was smart of you to put it in paper. I thought something good would come to you."

"It sure did, Mr. Speets. Now I can look as good as the other kids."

Walking to school in that new dress the next day felt like what I had heard about Christmas morning. I don't remember a single Christmas, but that day was magic. I forgot about the war and the Nazis, and I walked into the classroom clean and proud. During the streetcar ride, everyone wanted to sit by Mr. Speets, so every two minutes we traded places to have a turn next to him. Finally he told us to stop bouncing around and stay put until we got to the museum. I wanted to see all the new scenery out the window, but mostly I just looked down with pleasure at my blue and white lap.

I remember our footsteps echoing in the tall galleries of the museum and trying to be very quiet. Only one painting left a lasting impression on me. It showed several doctors standing around a boy who was tied down to a table. The doctors had knives in their hands and the boy looked very sick and frightened. I found Mr. Speets and pulled him over to the painting. "Mr. Speets, what are they going to do to that boy?" I asked.

"Well, Cato, it looks like they're going to operate on him," he explained.

"But he's still awake," I said with concern.

"He is, Cato, but he has some sickness inside of him and the doctors want to make him better by cutting it out," he tried to reassure me.

"But it would hurt bad, wouldn't it?" I remembered the stinging pain from my fall off the truck and shuddered.

Mr. Speets smiled, "That's why they have him tied down, so when it starts to hurt real bad, he can't get away."

"But that's mean!" I yelled. My voice echoed off the marble walls and everyone stared at me. "Why didn't they put him to sleep?"

"Shhh, Cato." Mr. Speets replied sternly, and then went on more gently. "I don't think doctors back then had found anything to put people to sleep before they operated."

I had an idea. "Mr. Speets, when I get out of school, I'm going to study real hard and see if I can help people when they have operations!" Little did I know that someday I would become a nurse. And how could I know that I would see that boy's expression of terror on thousands of faces, young and old, alive and dead.

After we were finished looking through the museum, we rode the streetcar to Mr. Speets's house for lemonade and homemade cookies. I wondered if he knew how lucky he was to live in such a clean house. After the streetcar ride back to school, I walked home reluctantly. I hated for it all to end. As I opened the front door, I did my best to smile at Ma. I started to tell her about everything we had done that day,

"That's nice, Cato," she said without looking at me. "Now I want you to go down to the bar and get your pa home."

"Can't I at least tell you what we did today?" I pleaded. "I want to tell you about all the things we saw."

"Not now, Cato!"

"Gosh, Ma, why not?" I wanted to know.

"Cato, don't talk back, get up to the bar and tell your father that your Oma has been taken to the hospital."

Shock took my breath away. "Ma, what's wrong with Oma? Is she going to die?"

"I don't know, Cato, now hurry up and get your father."

Breathless with fear, I ran to get my father. I raced as fast as I could, forgetting the new dress, the museum, and the happiness I had felt just minutes before. I ran inside the bar, panting, and had to squint in the darkness to find Pa. He was sitting at the bar talking with a woman.

"Pa, you got to get home. Oma's sick and had to go the hospital. Ma says to come home now." He didn't seem to hear me.

"Please Pa," I urged him, "let's go home." I grabbed at his limp hand as he turned to the woman beside him and slurred, "Lienie, this is my little girl, Cato." He looked at me with the drunken stare I detested and said, "Cato, say hello to my best friend, Lienie." I thought he would fall off his stool.

"Oh, hello," I said without quite looking at her, although I could see she was thin and dark-haired. "Pa, come home before Oma dies."

"She's not going to die," he said, wobbling on the bench. I started to cry.

"Pa," I almost screamed, feeling helpless and small, "come home!"

He finally gave in and stumbled toward the door. He waved to his friend, "See you another time, Lienie."

"Okay," she called, "but come back after you check on your mother-in-law."

He couldn't walk straight, and I was ashamed to be with him. "You better get sober, Pa, because they won't let you in the hospital if you're drunk," I said as I tried to prop him up.

"Who says your Pa is drunk?" he laughed. "I'm as sober as a skunk."

"Oh sure, Pa." How could we hurry when he could hardly walk? A block later, I asked him, "Pa, who is that woman, Lienie? Is she the whore Ma yells at you about?"

"Cato, I'm surprised you say things like that," he said, but he didn't deny it. I was tired of helping him, but we were almost home. As we approached the door, he mumbled, "Let's not talk about Lienie, okay?"

He almost fell through the door when we got home and tried to sound charming through his blurred voice. "Hello, my darling, my Tina. What's wrong with your mother? Is she sick?"

Ma spoke viciously to him. "Shut your drunken face. She's had a heart attack and been taken to the hospital." Ma's sudden tears shocked me—I had always thought she was too tough to cry. "You'd better get some coffee in you so you can sober up," she half screamed, half sobbed. After Pa had some coffee and cake his walking problem cleared up considerably.

"Ma, can I go to the hospital to see Oma?" I begged.

"No, Cato, they don't let kids in the hospital," she said.

"But she's my Oma!" I cried.

Opening the door to leave, she turned around and snapped, "I don't make the rules, Cato. Your father and I are leaving."

After they left, I sat in that quiet house, alone with my thoughts of Grandmother. I tried to imagine what it would be like not to have her to run to. Who would hold me and stroke my hair and tell me I was pretty? Where would I escape the torments of home? If God was real, how could he take her from me? I could feel in my heart that something bad was going to happen to my grandmother.

A couple of hours later, my folks came back home and Ma slumped into a chair and covered her face with her hands. Her whole body shook as she told me tearfully, "Cato, your Oma died."

"But she can't die," I said, trying to blink back my own tears.

"There's not a thing you can do about it. Now run over to Annie's house and tell Derk," she said. I needed her arms around me at that moment, but Pa practically pushed me out the door. I found my comfort in Derk's arms. He and Annie let me stay at her house and cry until I couldn't cry anymore. I was heartbroken over losing my grandmother. Ma never cried again about her mother, and we never talked about her death.

Because my mother was the oldest child in the family, Oma's coffin sat on two sawhorses in our living room for three days. Two men came and hung black curtains around the windows, over all the pictures in the living room, and around the casket. I watched it all from my hiding place in the corner. I stared and stared at that wooden box with the glass lid. When Ma and Pa left the room, I couldn't resist it. I sneaked up to the box and peeked over the side. There I met death for the second time in my life.

My grandmother was lying white and still. I felt bound by her stillness and could not pull myself away. Her hands were as gnarled as tree branches, her skin hung lifeless on her face. I wanted to touch her, shake her, anything to get her to wake up and smile at me. I noticed something sticking out of her neck. Looking around to make sure no one was coming, I lifted the glass just a little and reached in to pull on whatever it was. I had a piece of straw in my hand! I dropped the lid in a panic and ran to the kitchen where my mother was slumped in a chair.

"Ma, Ma," I screamed. "They stuffed my Oma with straw!"

Ma sat up like a shot. "What are you talking about?" she yelled at me with her eyes blazing.

I held the piece of straw before her and gasped, "I opened up her casket and I found . . ."

She cut me off crossly and tried to grab me, "You did what? You nasty child!"

Dodging her reach, I went on in a torrent. "I opened up the casket where Oma's sleeping, and this straw was sticking out of her neck!" I thought she should know they had done this terrible thing to my grandma.

"Oh, Cato, how could you do something like that?" Ma groaned. Derk happened to be there with my folks and tried to defend me.

"Mother, don't get mad at Cato. She was just curious, weren't you, little sister?" he said. I ran to his side in fear of Ma's wrath.

"I'll knock the curiosity out of you, Cato!" she growled.

"No, mother, you're not going to beat her. Stay by me, Cato." He held me on his lap for the first time in years and Ma backed off.

"I'm sorry," I said. "I didn't mean to do it, but how come Oma has straw inside of her?" Derk tried to explain to me that they had cut my grandmother open to find out why she died and then had stuffed her with straw to make her look better.

I stared at my brother, "Are you crazy?"

"Don't worry, Cato, it didn't hurt Oma because she can't feel anything when she's dead."

"But they shouldn't do that do her." I said. This whole experience was starting to make me feel sick. "How long will she be at our house?" I asked Derk. "I don't like having a dead person here." By this time, Piet had wandered into the room and started to tease me.

"You know, Cato, Oma isn't going to get out of the casket," he taunted.

"I know that, stupid," I shot back. "I just don't like it with a dead person in the house."

I checked on my grandmother every time I walked through the front room for the three days she was there. By the last day, her skin was starting to turn black and I didn't want to see her anymore. The two men came back with two carriages pulled by huge black horses with white plumes on their heads. They loaded the casket on one of the carriages.

I could hardly bear to wear my precious new dress for such a sad occasion, but it was better than wearing my old one. As Derk, Piet, and I finished getting ready, I asked my mother, "Are we going to get a ride in the buggy, too?" I was ready for some fun.

"Yes," she answered, shaking her fist at me, "and you kids better be good and not fight."

"Well, what about you and Pa? You better not fight, either," I declared. Ma slapped me hard across the mouth.

"Why did you do that?" I demanded as I shrunk from her fury.

"For having such a smart mouth, young lady. Now behave yourself!" she ordered. "And hurry up!"

As I pulled myself into the carriage, I heard Pa say, "You know that daughter of mine is getting to be more of a rebel every day." I couldn't tell if he was proud or disgusted. In the first buggy were Ma, Pa, Uncle Cor, and my blind aunt. Derk, Piet, and I rode in the second one. On the long, bumpy ride, my lip stung from Ma's slap and my heart ached for my grandmother.

The enormous hole at the cemetery seemed too deep and dark for Oma. I wanted her to be where there was light. "Are they going to put Oma in that hole?" I asked as I peered into its depths.

Good old Piet answered in his familiar mocking tone, "Of course they are, but then she's going to rot away in there."

"I know that," I told him pompously, "And she's going to have worms crawling out of her too, and they'll get into bed with you when you're asleep because you're a mean kid!" I took delight in his sudden terror as he clung to Derk.

"Is that true, Derk, what she tells me?" Piet asked with wide eyes.

"Of course, not, Piet." He gave me his sternest look but winked as he said, "Now stop teasing your brother, Cato!" The rest of the day we didn't have to go back to school because we were in mourning for my grandmother. Ma went home for coffee and sweets, and Pa went back to the bar, so Derk and I went for a walk along the canal and talked about Oma's death. As usual, Piet simply disappeared.

CHAPTER NINE

Whether we wish it or not we are involved in the world's problems, and all the winds of heaven blow through our land.

WALTER LIPPMANN, *A PREFACE TO POLITICS*

"How would you two like to have some pet rabbits?" Pa asked Piet and me one spring day. A question like that from our Pa was as surprising as finding money on the sidewalk. Piet and I figured there must be a trick.

"Really, Pa? You mean it?" Piet asked, his eyes narrow with doubt.

"You bet I mean it. We'll get some wood out of the cellar and make some cages if you promise to feed them," Pa answered. "And," he added with a wink, "you have to keep the cages clean." Piet and I looked at each other with happy disbelief. What had happened to Pa? He was never like this. Fearful that he would change his mind, we scrambled down the cellar stairs. From Pa's pile of wood scraps, we dug out broken pieces that Pa sawed into the right size. Pa didn't get mad for once, and I thought it must be a dream. Piet and I pounded the nails, and before long we carried the cages proudly up the stairs and out into our little yard.

Pa then walked us the few blocks to a friend's house. I had seen Pa with men in the bar, but I didn't think of them as friends. This man slapped Pa on the back and shook our hands and took us into his yard. The tiny baby rabbits captured my heart the instant I saw them. Piet chose two black rabbits and I chose two pure white ones, the same color as Mollie. The softness of their fur against my cheek was no dream. I slept outside by their cages that night just to be close to them.

As soon as school was out the next day, I talked Greet into coming home with me, telling her all about the new pets. I made her run all the way.

"Aren't they pretty?" I asked, snuggling a white rabbit tightly to my chest.

As she reached to touch it, her blue eyes grew suspicious behind her round glasses. "Are you raising those rabbits so you can eat them?" she asked.

"Oh, no, I will never do that," I answered as I nearly hugged the breath out of the rabbit. But fear shot through me like a sword. Was this Pa's trick?

"They sure poop a lot, don't they," I laughed nervously as I kicked at the dark round droppings on the ground. An idea hit me.

"Hey, I just thought of something, Greet," I said with mischief in my eyes. "You know that mean substitute teacher we have while Mr. Speets is sick?"

Greet wrinkled her nose in disgust and shuddered, "You mean Mrs. VanFleet?"

I nodded. "Yeah, I don't like her do you? Let's pull a trick on her!" Greet gave me her "now what?" look, but before I could explain, Ma came out and, ignoring Greet, told me to take a dress she had made to a lady down the street. At the sight of Ma, Greet slipped away as fast as she could, and I reluctantly obeyed Ma's request and put the rabbit back into its cage.

The "depression" Pa had told us about got worse after the invasion. The only thing I liked about it was that my father was not getting drunk every day. He was still drinking, but not as much as before. One night, though, he got so drunk he brought his girlfriend Lienie home with him to meet Ma. Ma screamed and started throwing everything within reach. Dishes shattered against Pa, the wall, the floor—this time he was too drunk to catch anything. It turned into such a clawing, cursing, ugly fight that it seemed even worse than the time Ma tried to stab Pa. Lienie watched in a stupor. Before long, Ma ran out of things to throw and just went limp, like a puppet with cut strings. She dragged herself upstairs to bed, turning to shake her fist at Pa and utter one more obscenity. After that night, Pa started drinking heavily again. I wondered where he found the money. Almost every day Ma would ask him how his whore was doing, and the fighting would erupt all over again.

One day Ma sent Piet and me over to the bar to pick up Pa. I had been inside before to sit on Pa's lap and eat liverwurst. There was always a woman sitting next to him. Pa had his bicycle there and we thought he could ride it home. While Piet steadied the bike, I tried to put one of his long legs over the middle bar and hoist his heavy body up. He fell off on the other side, almost toppling Piet over. I ran around and pushed him up again and he fell over the other side. We tried and tried but couldn't get him up. I got mad and started to cuss when Piet broke out giggling. I took one look at Piet, and we both collapsed on the sidewalk laughing so hard I almost peed my pants. Pa sat next to us in a daze. I finally told Piet to hang on to one side and I'd hang on to the other side, and we'd see if we could push him home.

"I've never seen him this drunk," Piet said.

"Well, I have," I groaned, stumbling as Pa fell toward my side. "There he goes again!" I yelled. "Hold on, Piet!" Piet was laughing, I began singing, and Pa fell right off the bike and sat down in the middle of the street. Piet and I laughed until tears ran down our cheeks. "Pa, you sure are funny when you're drunk," I told him as I poked at his chest.

"Oh," he slurred, "You think so, heh?"

"Can you get back up on your bike?" I asked.

"I don't know, kids. Just help me up. I can walk."

So Piet wheeled the bike and I led Pa by the hand as he stumbled toward home. It's a good thing Ma wasn't home when he got there. I got Pa sat down in a chair and then left for Sonja's house.

While Germany was trying to cripple Holland, I was busy trying to help Sonja learn how to walk.

"Did you know that I stood alone for almost five minutes yesterday?" she beamed when I got there. I forgot Pa in her grin of joyful triumph.

"Let's get started with your exercise again," I said as I grabbed her hands eagerly. "I want you to leave the wheelchair on one side of the street and try to walk across the street with me!"

She looked at me doubtfully. "You really are a dreamer, Cato. I don't think I can do that much yet."

"Yes, you can. Just think positive. I'll walk backwards in front of you and hold your hands. If you start to fall, I'll catch you." I pushed her to the edge of the street and helped her out of her wheelchair. What faith she had in me as we stood there clinging to each other. We took the first step and I knew how to distract her. "Did I tell you about the trick I'm going to pull on our substitute teacher," I asked. She shook her head, still holding tight to my arms. "Greet and I are going to get some of the rabbit poop out of my cages and pass it out as candy." She rolled her eyes and kept walking. I went on, "We're going to roll the stuff in flour or something. I'm going to let Mrs. Van Fleet take one first, and she'll get a mouthful of you know what." We were laughing like crazy and she was crossing the street without me holding on. "I can't stand that woman," I chuckled as I realized that Sonja didn't know she had let go.

We made it across the street and she couldn't believe it. I made her hold on to the lamp post and went back for her wheelchair. As I helped her settle into her chair, her first words were, "I don't like Mrs. VanFleet either, Cato, but I think your trick is too mean."

"Just promise me you won't tell anyone." She agreed to keep our secret and I wheeled her home.

One morning our substitute teacher, Mrs. VanFleet, gave us the stern look we despised and announced that Mr. Speets was almost over his illness and would be back in a few days. From two rows away Greet turned toward me with a look of alarm. Time was running out for the rabbit poop scheme we had been cooking up. Greet rushed up to me at lunch and pulled me away from the other girls. "Are you sure you want to go ahead with our trick, Cato?" she asked with her "I dare you" look. "We're going to get in a lot of trouble, you know."

"What the heck! I'm always in trouble at home so it doesn't matter if I'm in trouble at school," I said. I gave her a threatening glare, "You're not backing out on me, are you?"

"Oh, no," she quickly reassured me as she pulled me back toward the chattering group of girls.

Greet and I prepared our concoction that day after school. We selected only the moist soft rabbit droppings (we called them the "delicious" ones) that would hold the flour we rolled them in and lined them in neat rows to dry in the sun. Before I went to bed, I packed them in an old red candy tin of Ma's and hardly slept for the anticipation. I left for school earlier than usual, before Ma could ask any questions about her tin. Greet met me excitedly with a knowing glance and a nervous giggle. About ten minutes into class, I raised my hand and with my most practiced innocence, said sweetly, "Mrs. VanFleet, today is my mother's birthday and she said I could bring some candy to school to share with the class."

The teacher smiled so kindly I almost backed down. "Well, that is very nice of you and your mother. Cato, you may pass it around to the class after recess." Why did she have to be so sweet and polite about it? Oh, well, I thought, if she could be sweet and mean at the same time, then so could I.

After recess, she announced, "Children, Cato has some candy that she would like to pass out." I took the tin of rabbit droppings from my desk and cast a wink at Greet, who had an unbelievably large grin on her face. I walked properly to the front of the class. "Ma'am, my mother says I am to be polite and give the first piece to the teacher," I said with all the charm I could muster. Mrs. VanFleet took a piece and I noticed as she put it in her mouth that she didn't have her false teeth in.

I turned away just in time to hear her muffled voice ask, "What kind of candy is it, Cato? It tastes kind of funny." Greet broke out laughing first and I just couldn't keep a straight face. The teacher seemed to have actually swallowed the "candy." "What's the matter with you girls?" she asked suspiciously. We were laughing so hard we just could not answer. Now she was mad! She grabbed Greet by the collar, demanding, "You will tell me immediately what it is!"

Greet burst out, "It's rabbit shit!" There aren't words to describe the face Mrs. VanFleet pulled. No one could duplicate it. She made awful retching sounds and I thought she would throw up right there on the floor. Instead she bolted for the door and disappeared.

The rest of the class wanted to get in on the joke, too, and when we told them what we had done, they cheered and clapped. Our celebration was brought to a sudden end when the principal appeared in the doorway in his SS uniform, madder than a hornet.

"Sit down!" he thundered. He stormed to the front of the class. The veins on his neck stood out like cords. "Which one of you did that horrible thing to Mrs. VanFleet?" No one answered. He waited and waited, still not a sound. I stared at my desk, afraid to look up.

Abruptly he went on, "Very well, then you will all stay after school. I will write a sentence on the board and you will take out your paper right now and copy it 200 times."

As the chalk began to scrape on the blackboard, a boy's voice called out from somewhere behind me, "That's not fair! We shouldn't be punished for something someone else does." I stiffened. I knew he was right.

"All right, then, if you will tell me who did it, you will not be punished." the principal said. I felt the eyes of the world on me as I heard footsteps approaching my desk. The kid stood right by me and pointed his finger at me, "Cato did it."

"Cato, come up here," the principal's voice boomed. I walked reluctantly forward, eyes down. He put his hand under my chin and made me look at him. His voice bored into me, "Is it true what you did to Mrs. VanFleet?" I stared at his red face and the swollen veins on his neck and suddenly the look on Mrs. VanFleet's face flashed through my mind. I burst out laughing again. "Cato," he said, as if he were handing down a sentence to a criminal, "You will go and stand in the corner for the rest of the day, the whole day. You shall not eat your lunch, no recess, no break, nothing. You will stay there until school is out." For once speechless, I went to the corner. Mrs. VanFleet came back in the room without a word to me or any mention of the candy incident.

At the end of the longest day of my life, the principal returned and asked me if I was tired of standing in the corner. "No, sir," I replied sweetly. I would rather lie than admit that my legs were itchy and weak, my back ached and I had to go to the bathroom so bad I thought I would split.

He looked at me harshly, but his voice was calm, "Cato, you will go home now. You are being expelled from school for one week. During that time you will do the homework I give you. I want both your parents to come to school so that I can tell them what you have done. Do you understand me?"

"My father won't come because he's always drunk, and I don't think my mother will come, either," I told him curtly. My folks at school? What a joke.

He wagged his finger under my nose, "You just make sure they come."

So I took my candy tin home and didn't say a word to anyone. Every morning for the next week, I pretended to go to school, but hid around the corner. When Ma left, I sneaked back inside and climbed on the roof to do my homework until Piet came home from school. The principal must have decided it wasn't worth the trouble to try and get my folks to school. And I sure wasn't going to help him.

Mollie and my two white rabbits gave me a wordless comfort no human could. On our rooftop perch, Mollie curled up next to me and purred as I told her everything that was happening to me. When the fury of my home got to be too much for me, instead of running away every time, I would sit on a little stack of bricks in our backyard with the rabbits nestled in my lap. They gave me the kind of peace Oma had taken with her when she died. As I stroked their heads, their ears lay back and they became very calm. I felt like a different girl—a gentle, loving one. The creatures' utter harmlessness enchanted me and soothed the turmoil in my soul. Somehow they worked their way inside and found a tender place in my hard little heart. On many an afternoon, they brought a bit of contentment to my threatening world.

Pa interrupted my reverie one afternoon with the shocking announcement, "We better not let those rabbits get too old or they won't make good stew. It's about time to butcher them."

"What are you talking about? You can't do that to our pets." My rage exploded. "They're my rabbits and you better not touch them." I couldn't stand or run with a lap full of rabbits. I could only shout at him as he turned to go in the house, "You're the meanest man I know!"

So there was a trick after all. He had meant to eat them all along. Maybe I would have felt differently if he had told us when he got us the rabbits what his intentions were—that he was just planning to fatten them up so we could cook them. I got up as quickly as I could, put the rabbits back into their cage, and ran into the house. I found Pa at the kitchen table. "Please, Pa, don't kill my rabbits," I begged. "I love them. Maybe Piet doesn't care that much, but I do."

"Stop it, Cato, you know how hard it is to get meat with the war on." He looked at me with no feeling, as if I were a stranger. I felt even more helpless against his stony face than against his wrath. I walked back outside, cold with fear.

Not long after that Piet and I went outside one morning to feed our pets and were stunned to see my two white rabbits hanging by their ears from the clotheslines, their throats slashed. Bright red blood stained their white fur. I stood numb, unable to speak. I felt as if I had been stabbed, as if my life were bleeding out of me. Blinded by the bright sun and the gruesome sight, I thought I would pass out. A sob rose in my throat, shaking my whole body. My two beautiful pets, my beautiful friends, were dead!

Anger suddenly caught up with my shock, and I raged through the back door screaming for Pa. He and Ma stood in the kitchen, as if waiting to see what I would do. Hurling swearwords, I lunged at him and pounded him with my fists with every ounce of strength I had. Pa had a tough time pushing me away as he yelled back, "Grow up, Cato! There's a war on and what's done is done! Get on to school."

"I hate you, Pa! And I hate you, Ma, for letting him do it!" I spat at them. "One of these days I'm going to kill you for this and run away." Pa held me at arm's length, but I still clawed at him like the tomcats I had seen tearing at each other in the street. Ma screamed at me to shut up, and I felt myself go limp from despair and exhaustion. As I fell onto a chair, I could only whimper, "You're going to have to pay for what you did. How does it feel to be hated by your own kids?"

That did it. My father slammed his fist into my cheek and sent me reeling off the chair. "Don't you ever talk to me that way again," he screamed.

From the floor, I gathered enough strength to yell back, "I'll talk to you like that any time I feel like it. I hate you more than anything!" My cheek burned with pain, my body seethed with hate for Pa. I half crawled, half stumbled toward the door and spat all my anger and hate into one last sentence, "I hope you choke on the meat and die when you eat it!"

I cried more tears that day than I had ever cried in my life. I was late for school and couldn't find the words or strength to talk to Mr. Speets. All I could see in my mind were glassy eyes and blood-stained fur. After school, Ma and Pa were gone and I talked Greet into helping me take Piet's little black rabbits to a field at the edge of town to let them go. I wept again as I watched them scamper to freedom, grimly determined that I would never forgive Pa for what he did to my pets.

CHAPTER TEN

Fear was my father, Father Fear.
His look drained the stones.

THEODORE ROETHKE, *THE LOST SON*

By the spring I turned ten, in 1941, we knew what buildings the Germans lived in and we knew the people who had become traitors to their own country because they hung red German flags with swastikas from their windows. Black markets were popping up all over the city where you could buy food for outrageously high prices. The Germans didn't allow us to have heat in our homes. With little food and no heat, the winter cold went right to our bones.

I still didn't understand what the Germans had against the Jews. Jews were made to wear yellow armbands with "Jood" printed on them. The soldiers' blaring loudspeakers commanded us in hate-filled voices to stay away from Jews. I was not supposed to play with my next-door friends, Hans and Jopie. Of course, I did anyway. I sneaked the back way over the roof whenever I could. I'd made up my mind that no German was going to tell *me* what I could do.

Whenever Greet and I walked along a main street, we held onto each other tightly because of the soldiers everywhere. One spring afternoon, a break in the rain and the unusually warm weather lured us outside. As we admired the new tulips and tried to forget the war, roaring laughter interrupted our brief joy. It was the piercing, mean laughter of a taunting crowd of men. Only a few yards from us a circle of towering German soldiers had formed around an old Jewish man. We saw one soldier standing tall and proud inside the circle, chuckling as the Jew was forced to lick the Nazi's boots and then polish them dry with his beard. The old man seemed so small and broken, the soldiers as frightening as beasts. Greet and I forgot the flowers and ran home.

Posters appeared stapled to trees and poles with the words *Verboden voor Joden* (Forbidden for Jews). Many times I saw Jews thrown down in the streets and spat upon. I saw Jews waiting in line to get into big German trucks. Voices coming through the loudspeakers promised them they would be going to better places to live. We heard rumors later about "concentration camps," but of course at that time, we had no idea what a concentration camp was. Greet's mother told us we were both lucky to have blonde hair and light blue eyes. "You are the kind of girls Germans like," she said. She called it lucky, but it sounded very bad to me.

Airplanes flew over our city, dropping hundreds of bombs. Bomb shelters were built beneath the bridges where people could hide when the air raid siren sounded. The sirens always spooked me—they sounded like the wavering wail of something dying. Pa put tape in squares over all our windows. He said that if a bomb exploded close by, the glass from the windows would stick to the tape and not shatter all over the house. Since we were not allowed to have any electricity, we mixed water and oil in a fishbowl and Pa fixed up a wick to float in it. That was all the light we had. Then orders came to black out all the windows so no light would shine through. Pa hung blankets over all the windows. I guess the Germans were scared the city would be seen by the Allied forces.

Whenever the airplanes dropped bombs, I would duck, but I knew it was silly. You could get hit wherever you were standing. I watched the deadly black specks in the sky get bigger and bigger, knowing they would explode somewhere, maybe on me or my home or my school. The enemies I had faced before in my life could be screamed at, kicked, faced eye to eye, or at least run from. I hated this new enemy, this distant, anonymous, yet even more cruel enemy. Once the Allied air raids started, I knew the pilots were trying to destroy the Germans, but they didn't see who was hurt. They couldn't see my friends, my beloved teacher, or my Derk. They couldn't see me, watching the sky in terror, wondering if I would be the next to die.

Pa turned our basement into a shelter. He told us it was safer to be below ground during a bombing. Sometimes the bombing went on for hours and hours while we grew stiff and cold down in that cellar. When we finally heard the steady blast of the "all-clear" signal, Piet and I would race up the stairs and outside as fast as we could go. That is, until the day we ran outside and down to the canal. A bomb had hit the bridge. Pieces of wood and metal from the bomb shelter walls were everywhere, ragged and twisted. We stopped and stared. A human hand lay in the street, almost at our feet. Not far from it was a severed leg, still wearing a torn trouser leg, caked with blood. The more we looked, the more body parts we saw scattered in the debris. Piet let me take his hand and we turned and ran back home, terrified. So this was war.

After that, we stayed home after the bombs until the worst of the destruction was cleared away.

Not even the war kept Pa sober all the time. The year I turned eleven, Pa came after me again. Ma was invited to a special evening for actors and actresses at a local theater. She dressed up in a black dress and hat and strutted around like a peacock. She told us she would be home very late and not to stay up for her. We tried to stay awake anyway, but when we could hardly keep our eyes open, I climbed the stairs to go to bed and Piet pulled his bed down from the living room wall. I don't know how long I had been sleeping when I could feel someone pulling the blankets away and trying to curl up beside me. I heard my father's drunken voice whine, "Lienie, I want you."

I threw my blanket back, leapt up to turn on the light and saw my father stark naked in my bed. He pulled at me and I shouted, "It's me, Cato, your daughter." But he gripped my arm tightly, pulled me roughly onto the bed, and tried to push me over onto my back. My wrist burned in pain.

"I'm not Lienie," I screamed, trying to wiggle free. Somehow I managed to get away, and I cried hysterically as I ran downstairs to Piet.

"Piet! Wake up!" I shouted. "Help me! Wake up!" I shook his shoulders, fiercely whispering into his ear. As I shook him harder I realized that he was only pretending to be asleep. "Piet, come on, wake up! Pa's after me. He's in my bed!" I could hear Pa bellowing upstairs, "Lienie, come back!"

I heard heavy footsteps on the stairs, then coming closer and closer on the wooden floor of the hall. I slapped Piet hard across the cheek and he sat up with a start. "Ouch!" Piet growled. "What did you do that for?"

"Pa's coming after me!" I cried uncontrollably. Piet pushed me away with disinterest.

"Pa's too drunk to do anything. Go back to bed and leave me alone!"

I squeezed myself under Piet's bed just as Pa's huge shape darkened the doorway. I could see his feet as I scooted back toward the wall as far as I could, shivering as I tried to make myself invisible. My pounding heart pleaded, "Don't tell, don't tell, don't tell."

"Piet, have you seen Lienie?" Pa asked in a voice gruff yet filled with the heartbreak of a deserted child. Pa was crying! "Lienie ran away from me," he groaned through tears.

I felt the bed shake and saw Piet's feet hit the floor. Don't tell, don't tell! Holding my breath, I braced myself for Pa's wrath.

"C'mon Pa," I heard Piet try to soothe him. "Let me help you back up to bed."

"No, boy," Pa heaved. "It's all right. I've just got to find Lienie."

My heart was still racing as I watched Pa's feet turn toward the door and heard Piet say, "Lienie's not here, Pa, you must have been dreaming."

Maybe I had been dreaming. How could Pa come after me like this? He suddenly raised his voice in anger, "Don't you lie to me, boy, I know she was here."

Piet pushed him toward the door, "No, Pa, you have to go to bed. You have to get up early and go to work."

Please, Pa, I thought, listen to Piet and leave me alone.

Pa was still for a moment and then mumbled, "You're right." As I saw Pa and Piet go into the hall I went limp from exhaustion. The creaking of the floor overhead told me when Pa collapsed into his bed, and then Piet was back.

I crawled out from under his bed and fell into his arms, even though I knew he didn't like me to touch him. He hugged me quickly and then sat down on his bed. "You can go back to bed, Cato," he said matter-of-factly. "Pa isn't going to bother you anymore tonight. He's just drunker than usual."

"I'm never going back up there as long as he's there. You go sleep up there if you're so tough," I dared him.

"You're not sleeping in my bed, Cato." A fat lot he cared.

"Then I'll go sleep on the roof again."

"You better not, 'cause if Ma or Pa catches you, you're going to get it!"

"Then I'll just sleep under your bed!" I insisted, still trembling.

"Suit yourself, Cato, I'm going back to bed." He rolled over and made me get off his bed so he could pull the blanket up. I laid on his cold floor and soon heard him breathing heavily in sleep. It would be several hours before I could get back to sleep. I never told my mother about that night because I knew she wouldn't believe me or wouldn't care. Someday I would have a place with a bed and a room of my own I told myself. But that was far in the future for me.

I have experienced many kinds of fear in my life and still do not know which is the most terrifying. That night I knew the fear and disbelief that came when someone who should have loved and protected me suddenly turned his raging lust on me. I have known the paralyzing fear of bombs and other faceless horrors of war. I've known the panic of being beaten by strangers as if I were nothing more than a loathsome rat. And I have known the numb despair that almost broke my spirit when

I faced the truth of my most secret fear—that the universe was unaware of my suffering. How can I measure or compare these fears? What I do know is that the fear of my own father so bruised and crushed the fragile trust beginning to bud in my heart that I knew I would never feel safe in my home again.

From that time on, I slept on the roof with Mollie and felt a hard shell growing around me. I didn't know it then, but that shell would one day help keep me alive.

CHAPTER ELEVEN

*Older people have formed their opinions about everything
and don't waver before they act. It's twice as hard for us
young ones to hold our ground, and maintain our opinions,
in a time when all ideals are being shattered and destroyed,
when people are showing their worst side, and do not know
whether to believe in truth and right and God.*

ANNE FRANK

While our world crumbled around us, I spent a lot of time at Sonja's house, talking with her and trying to help her learn to walk. More than once I had chased kids off who had taunted her and called her a "cripple." I had to punch a few, but they deserved it.

Sonja and I could talk about anything. As I pushed her wheelchair slowly along the street one afternoon, everything about Pa spilled out before I knew what I was saying. "Aren't you scared of him, Cato?" she asked with deep concern in her eyes.

"Of course I'm scared. Why do you think I'm back to sleeping on the roof?"

"That's too dangerous. What if you fall?"

"Then I would make a big splash on the sidewalk," I laughed, slapping my hands together.

"Oh, stop joking about it," she said. "I just wish there was something I could do to help."

I knelt down in front of her wheelchair and looked straight into her eyes, "There is, Sonja. Just stay my friend."

Although no one was allowed to be on the streets after 8 P.M., Pa started going out during the night anyway to steal food from the Germans who had stolen farms from the Dutch people. He told us that deep down, the Germans were afraid of being outside in the dark because they knew they could be shot by the Dutch resistance. Behind the Germans' backs, we started calling them "Krauts."

The food Pa stole for us was not really enough to keep us going. He stole sugar beets Ma called "cow food," but she grated and mixed them with a little black-market flour to make pancakes. Still, our bellies were always growling. There was hardly anything to feed my cat. Mollie's ribs began to show through her fur, and her legs looked like chicken bones.

Pa joined a group that helped Jews who had been forced to live in a ghetto behind high brick walls. Members of the group printed false passports and two newspapers called *DE WAARHEID* (The Truth) and *TROUW* (Loyalty). Greet's father was also a member, and since he drove a streetcar, he was very good at distributing these newspapers. Pa's work against the Germans was the first thing that made me feel proud of him since he killed the rat in the cellar.

Pa let me help because I could squeeze my skinny body through places where bricks had been worked loose in the ghetto wall. Several times he sent me through the dark and smelly sewers to deliver pamphlets and false passports to a basement room in the ghetto. I liked the excitement of it and despite my feelings for Pa, it made me feel important.

There were also groups of Dutch men who wore white armbands with the letters NBS which stood for *Nederlandse Binnenlandse Strijdkrachten* (The Battle Group). Their duty was to help anyone who needed it. Pa told us to look for one of them if we ever needed protection. During the invasion, they had tried to stop the Germans from going over our bridges, and they were the ones who cleaned up the arms and the legs and helped the injured after the bombs. But, in time, like everyone else, they were getting weaker and weaker from the lack of decent food.

What would I have done without Greet? Together, the two of us dared to take risks I would never have taken alone. Many nights we sneaked out after curfew and met at the "Leidse Plein," one of Amsterdam's town squares. Then we furtively made our way to the part of town where the Germans and their "women" lived. We walked as close to the buildings as possible, dodging in and out of doorways, always watching. It was the Germans' garbage we were after and we worked quickly—the Nazis made sure their prostitutes had plenty to eat. Greet and I looked on porches and in yards, or sometimes the cans were just out on the sidewalk. We dumped the cans, then each took a side and rummaged through the mess for potato peelings, wilted lettuce, fruit, moldy vegetables. The rancid odor almost choked us.

How strange it was to celebrate the discovery of some crust of bread or half-rotten apple in that greasy filth as if we had found gold. We would have been ashamed of ourselves if we hadn't been so hungry. Whatever looked even close to edible we stuffed in our pockets or wrapped in an old napkin and then ran to the next garbage can. Leaving a trail of slimy garbage in the street gave me almost as much pleasure as finding something to eat. It didn't take us long to fill our pockets and race home to take a good look at our haul and try to fix it into some kind of a meal. Ma and Pa didn't ask any questions—they had a good idea where the food came from. Piet joined us sometimes in our scavenging.

On one of our raids, Greet and I found a can with the lid stuck tight. I held the can and as Greet tugged on the lid, it hit the street with a clanging noise. Suddenly a window was thrown open and a woman yelled, "What's going on down there? Get out of my garbage can!" Running like lightning, I couldn't resist the temptation to turn around and yell, "Shut up, you lousy Nazi whore!" Long-legged Greet was ahead of me and didn't bother to try to stop me.

After awhile, we started to develop sores all over our bodies. When they itched, we scratched with dirty fingernails, infecting the sores that grew bigger and bigger. We could only get one small bar of soap with our food coupons. We called it "airplane soap" because it would float on top of the water, but would not make any suds. No one could get clean with it, and everyone had lice and fleas. The lice burrowed into our open sores and festered. Pa soaked old towels in petroleum and wrapped them around our heads for about half an hour. Then he took his tweezers and picked dead lice one by one out of our oozing sores. Every time he dug one out, I sat straight up against the searing pain and shouted, "Another dead kraut, Pa!"

Word had spread that the church nearby was giving free meals to members of the congregation on Wednesday nights. We weren't members, but I told Piet that maybe someone would recognize our faces from the few times Ma took us there. It worked. I did some cleaning in exchange for food. It also gave me a chance to sneak down into their cellar and stuff a few potatoes into my apron pocket. I knew it was stealing, but everyone stole who didn't want to die. I remembered the saying, "God helps those who help themselves." So I helped myself.

I saw this man Adolf Hitler many times. He stood in plazas ranting and raving like Pa at his worst. I could understand most of what he said from the German I learned in school and from being surrounded by German soldiers. He screamed until his veins stood out on his neck about how the Jews were to blame for all the problems in the world, how he wanted to have only pure people living on the earth. He had a certain look in his eyes that seemed to hypnotize people. Women threw flowers at Hitler's feet. People went hysterical screaming "Heil Hitler! Heil Hitler!," pushing people out of the way to try to get a better view. I didn't like to get close because I didn't want to get crushed. If people didn't raise their hands, the guards beat them with rifles or slammed into them with their heavy boots. I tried to make sense of all the things I heard people saying about Hitler. I heard that he had been born in Austria and had wanted to be an artist, that his father was an alcoholic, and that his mother died when he was nineteen years old. I heard he was wounded in World War I and that he wanted to rule the whole world. People whispered that he was killing gypsies and black people and that he was having cruel experiments done on the mentally retarded. The funny thing was that people said that Hitler was part Jew, but he wouldn't admit it.

We also heard talk of a man called Fritz Sauckel who had been rounding up thousands of Dutch people and sending them to labor camps to "help the war effort." These were non-Jews whom Sauckel promised good working conditions, high pay, and paid vacations. If that didn't convince them, he threatened to cut off food coupons to their families. Sauckel was in close contact with Hitler at all times—he was another cold-blooded killer. Rumors claimed that by the end of 1942, Sauckel had sent half a million Dutchmen away against their will. Derk was one of them. He was rounded up and sent to Germany before the reports came back that the work camps were nothing but prisons with quarters like dog kennels where the men had to crawl around like animals.

Derk was gone before I could say good-bye to him. From that point on, my hate for Hitler became a very personal one.

After the Nazis had confiscated our radio, Pa concocted a home-made one out of a plank of wood, old radio tubes, a screw here, a wire there, whatever he could find. He got so mad trying to get it to work, he threw it on the floor and it started to play. From then on, he turned it on by touching two of the wires together and hid it behind the front board of one of the stairs to the cellar. Whenever he thought it was safe to listen, he took it from its hiding place and we huddled real close to find out the latest news.

One day we heard that the Americans would soon be having a food drop. By this time, the Germans provided only enough ration coupons to give a family of four two pounds of potatoes and half a loaf of bread to last a week. The schools were turned into *Gaarkeukens* (kitchens), where we stood in line for hours waiting for a ladle of watery soup to be poured into our small pans. When we heard about the food drop, we let others know when it would be through the underground. Pa had us help him dig up all the tiles in our tiny yard and put the dirt in the coal bin. Of course the coal bin was empty because the Nazis wouldn't let us have any fuel. Pa's plan was for us to bury any food we could find and then cover the yard again with tiles.

On the night the American food drop came, people crowded onto the roofs of their homes. Piet and I stood on our neighbor's flat roof with a blanket around our shoulders, and our folks waited in the yard. This way if any of the food fell on the roof, we could throw it down to them and have them bury it immediately. The skies were very dark and Piet, who was not used to being on the roof, begged to go inside. "The Americans won't dare drop food to us with so many Germans around," he said. I knew he was scared.

"Don't be such a baby, Piet," I scolded him.

No sooner were the words out of my mouth than we could hear the low hum of airplanes. It seemed strange to look for hope in the sky when so much death had rained down on us, but there we were, hugging each other, with me yelling, "Here they come! They're going to drop food!"

"Shut up, Cato! You're going to wake up the whole neighborhood," Piet said.

"Oh, get lost. Look at the other roofs. There are lots of people on them. They aren't asleep!" I told him. Then the noise was too loud to hear each other as the black dots took the shape of planes. Everyone on the roofs was cheering, waving, jumping up and down. The airplanes swooped so low we could have sworn the people inside could see us. We could see what seemed like millions of little dots falling from the planes and disappearing between the buildings of Amsterdam. Large square cans fell on the roofs and into the yards. We heaved the ones that landed on our roof over the side so Ma and Pa could cover them with sand, spread a tarp over them, and put the tiles back in place right away. After the planes had gone, Piet and I scampered down the neighbors' stairs to help with the work. Pa had us keep a few cans out so the Germans would see we had a few and not suspect anything.

That night we all sat in the living room with a great feeling of jubilation. Inside a can we found packages of dried potatoes, powdered eggs, crackers, cookies, and chocolate. We lit into the food with a gusto that came from weeks of eating scraps out of the Germans' garbage cans. I took Mollie on my lap and told her that she didn't have to go to bed hungry because we had lots of food in the house now. I talked to that cat as if she were a human being. Our yard looked a bit higher because of all that food being buried, but no one could guess there were cans below the tiles. In all we had collected thirty-seven cans.

The next day it was announced that the soldiers were going to search every house and take whatever food the Allies had dropped the night before. "Those swine," Pa said. "Don't they ever give up?" Two nights later, a pounding on the door startled us.

German voices boomed, "Open this door!" As Pa opened the door, two German soldiers pushed their way inside, shouting "Heil Hitler!"

Pa mumbled some sort of answer.

"Where is the food the Americans dropped?" they demanded.

"What food?" Pa said. "We don't have any food."

They shoved him to the side and walked through our home as if it belonged to them, poking inside closets and cupboards. We hardly dared breathe as they went down into our little yard. They couldn't tell that it was higher than usual. Of course they took the three cans they found upstairs. Ma's face was ashen as they again raised their hands to salute Hitler and abruptly left. "Pa," I asked, "what would they have done if they had found any more food?"

He responded somberly, "I'd rather not tell you, Cato."

I never got used to the long, wailing moans of the air raid sirens. They were getting on everyone's nerves. The bombings were so frequent and had become so terrible that whenever I was in bed or in the cellar, I would just curl up into a tight knot, hoping that no one could see me. I remember standing in front of the bedroom window when the screeching of the sirens startled me. My skin crawled and I felt as if my body were turning inside out. I heard Pa calling for me to get down into the basement. I hated to be in that cellar. I felt like a mole living beneath the ground. What if the dirt piled on top of me and smothered me? What if the bombs destroyed the world and I was forced to live under the ground for the rest of my life? What if . . . ?

"Cato! Get down here right now!" Pa yelled urgently.

"I'm coming, Pa," I called. I squeezed Mollie a little too hard, and she let out a pitiful mew as I carried her downstairs. Mollie squirmed to get out of my clutches as I hurried for the cellar. I could tell by the sound of the explosions that the bombs were falling closer. Ma and Piet were already there. Pa gave me a kick in the bottom before he bolted the door and came down to sit by us. Suddenly we could feel the house shaking as a thunderous explosion sounded directly over our heads. We felt a terrible trembling and heard the shattering of dishes and banging sounds of things falling apart upstairs. I covered my ears and started to scream, "Pa, Ma, we've been hit! We're going to die!" My eyes were shut tight, but I felt blinded by fire. My throat burned with screams I couldn't stop. Over and over they came. I was sure death had found me.

Pa's hard slap on my face silenced me. Reaching for my cheek, I asked through tear-filled eyes, "Why did you hit me, Pa? I wasn't doing anything."

"You were getting hysterical, Cato!"

Mollie had jumped from my arms and was cowering in the corner. Piet hung on Pa's arm whimpering, "Pa, did we get hit?"

"I think so, Piet. Keep still and when the all-clear siren turns on we can go upstairs and see." In the dark, I could see Ma sitting on a stump, head down, trying to pull herself into a little ball. She sat silent and trembling.

After what seemed like days, the short blast of the all-clear sirens sounded and Pa stood at the cellar door. Before he let us out he warned sternly, "Don't touch anything that looks strange because it could be some ammunition from the bomb that landed." Pa moved the heavy bolt back and opened the cellar door. In spite of our eagerness to get upstairs, we moved slowly, dreading what we might discover. Pa growled curses. I soon saw why. Pieces of glass were everywhere; pictures had fallen from the walls; chairs lay on their sides; Piet's bed had broken off the wall. Most of the glass had been blasted from the blanket-covered windows, but Pa's tape had kept it from breaking into even smaller pieces. It was as if the heavens had shattered, with all the stars in ruins at our feet.

We stood there in shock for the longest time. Finally, without a word, I picked up the picture of Derk and placed it on the kitchen counter because the mantel shelf from above the stove was lying on the floor. His eyes seemed to look at me with a longing to come home. I wondered for the first time if he was better off where he was. As we began to dig through the rubble, trying to clean up, it felt as though we were moving in some slow motion trance. Nothing seemed real. Pa said, "We can't get any glass so I'll nail wood over the windows. It will keep us warmer, anyway."

I could hear people outside calling for their families. I walked through the mess to look out a paneless window and was stunned by the crumbled buildings, smoke from fires, and dazed people. We had been lucky. Homes down the street had been blown into splinters. The bombs had opened up huge holes in our neighborhood, so I could see homes on the next street I had never seen from our porch before. From what we heard on the radio and on the streets, those bombs came from the English and Americans. What's the matter with them? I thought. Couldn't they tell the difference between a Kraut and a Dutchman? They should have bombed the hotel where the Nazis lived with their Dutch whores, those traitors. One bomb could have taken care of them.

While I was helping clean up the disaster, I found the butcher knife Pa had tried to stab Ma with, the one I had tried to get away from him when he cut his hand. There was no trace of blood on it now. Gently I put it back in the drawer where it belonged.

Later that day I discovered that some of my neighbors were hurt, but none had been killed. As I walked along my street, I could see where bombs had blown apart floors and walls, so I could see right into people's cellars. I don't know how we all survived.

About this time we pleaded with Pa to teach us how to steal food from the Germans. I told him, "Pa, what if the Germans take you away? We don't know how to steal food from them and we'll starve." Pa had not had a drink in a long time now. His face looked so haggard, so old. Everyone looked awful. *Hunger odeum* had broken out—we had bloated bellies and arms and legs like sticks.

Pa brought home some dark fabric he picked up on the black market. He told Ma to get busy and make some outfits for us with hoods to cover our blonde hair. He promised that as soon as the outfits were finished, he would teach us how to steal food from the Germans at night. "Only it isn't really stealing," he insisted. "It is taking back from the Germans what they stole from us in the first place."

For the first time since my trip to the museum, Ma sewed something new for me. I normally wore hand-me-downs, but my black-hooded clothes fit just fine. Pa made us each a loop of wire and explained, "If you should ever come across a dog or a cat while you're out, it might make too much noise and give you away. Use this wire on its neck and kill it."

"But Pa, what if someone did that to Mollie," I protested.

"You can't let Mollie outside anymore because everyone is hungry. Someone could kill her and put her right into the pot," Pa warned.

"They better not touch my cat," I declared.

"Listen to me," Pa said. "If you find an animal, kill it and bring it home."

"I could never eat a cat or dog," I gagged. "Could you, Ma?"

"If you're hungry enough, you can learn to eat anything," she answered sadly.

Eventually, we went out with Pa many nights and rummaged for food, but I never used my wire.

CHAPTER TWELVE

*It is terrible outside. Day and night more of those poor
miserable people are being dragged off, with nothing but
a rucksack and a little money. Families are torn apart,
the Dutch people are anxious too, their sons are being
sent to Germany. Everyone is afraid.*

ANNE FRANK

One night just after we had finished eating our sugar beet pancakes, we heard soft knocking on the front door. We knew it could not be soldiers, because they nearly broke doors down with their banging. Pa said, "I don't think I should answer the door; a person can't be too careful anymore." But the knocking became persistent. With Piet and me right behind him, Pa walked to the door and put his ear against it. Maybe it was a soldier trying to trick us after all. Just as he turned around, the knocking started again.

"Please," a voice whispered. "It is Isaak from next door." It was my friend the baker! Pa opened the door a tiny crack, and I heard Isaak's familiar voice, "Please, please let us in."

Pa whispered gruffly, "You know we are not allowed to have Jews in the house. Go away, before the Germans get here." He held the door firmly with his foot but didn't shut it in the baker's face.

Isaak's voice grew louder, "Please help us. We can hear the trucks around the corner from us picking up more Jews, and you know what will happen to us, don't you?"

Pa asked, "Did anyone see you come to my door?"

"No, no one has seen us. But the trucks are almost here."

Pa opened the door and there stood my friends from the bakery, Jopie and Hans, with their mother behind them. Their faces were painted with fear. Pa quickly pulled them inside and closed the door behind them. I knew we were in danger of a Nazi raid, of threats, beatings, humiliation, and possibly death. I wanted to help my friends, but I was overwhelmed with the fear that we would all be shipped off together. Then Hans smiled at me. In his crooked frightened smile was a mixture of heartache and hope. I knew then and there that I would do anything to get him away from Hitler's soldiers.

"Thank you, thank you. May you be blessed."

"Thank you, Isaak. Now what can I do for you?" Pa asked frantically.

"Please help us get away before the trucks find us. Do you have a back door that leads into another street?"

"Don't you remember there is no way out of our yard? I don't know how to help you folks get away from here." Pa's voice was tight, and he was running his hand through his hair. I could hear the sound of trucks and German voices getting closer but could not distinguish the words. They were the sounds of inescapable doom.

Pa turned to Isaak, who still stood quietly near the door, "This is hopeless. Isn't there someone else you can trust to help you get away?"

"No," he answered with great sorrow, "There isn't anyone else, sir." Hans and Jopie clung to their father listening, afraid to move.

"Pa," I said. "I got an idea."

"Hush, Cato, not now," Pa snapped.

"Please, Pa, it's a good idea."

"Please let Cato speak," Isaak said. "Maybe she's got something."

I hardly dared say it. "I'll tell you what, I could help them escape over the roof."

"That's ridiculous," my father interrupted.

Isaak raised his hand to silence Pa. "You know," he said, "that may not be a bad idea what your daughter is suggesting. Besides, there isn't anywhere else for us to go."

Pa looked at me doubtfully, "Cato, are you sure you can do it?"

"Sure I'm sure, Pa."

He turned to Isaak. "It's true. Cato knows her way around the roof." To me he added, "But I don't want you to take any chances. You know it's pitch dark outside. We better hurry before the Nazis find out we've got Jews in the house."

Pa showed them up the stairs. Everyone seemed surprisingly calm with no idea what a weight their trust put on my shoulders. Pa pulled down the ladder and climbed up into the dark attic first. Isaak led his family one by one to their last hope. I followed them into the attic and guided them over to my familiar window. We spoke as shadows in the night.

"I'm going to go first," I explained. "And don't talk when you get outside because your voice can really carry up here." I felt kind of important, doing this for them. "The hardest part is going to be jumping from our roof over to the flat one, but I'm positive you can do it. Just don't look down, whatever you do. It is only a small jump, maybe two feet. I know you can do it." What I didn't tell them, what I didn't even want to think about, was that I had never made that jump in the dark.

I went on, "Now, when you climb out of our window, go out backward, then lean forward against the roof and stand on the drainage gutter." I stood on a chair, slipped out the window, and found the gutter with my feet. A breeze blew my hair in my face, and I heard the grinding of trucks far below me. Isaak followed, slowly, struggling against his fear, each foot searching for stability. I could hear him softly mumbling. Was he praying? Then Pa passed Jopie through to her father. Dinie, the mother, and Hans followed, and there the five of us were, three floors up from the street, the trucks, and deportation. And two feet across nothing but air from possible safety.

Inch by inch, we made our way toward the end of the gutter, leaning against the roof. Turning, I gave a quick look around, and even I was a little bit scared of the jump. I closed my eyes and a picture of myself crumpled on the street below flashed through my mind.

"Now," I whispered, "we are at the end of this gutter and we have to jump across to that flat roof. I'll jump first. One at a time, turn around, lean with your back against the roof, then when you are ready lean forward and take a big long step. I'll grab you. Now watch me." With no choice but to jump, I threw myself across the chasm so hard I fell on my hands and knees, but I made it! I sat for a moment trying to get my breath back. Isaak reached for his little girl's hand. "Okay, Jopie, you're going first." I grabbed Jopie's shaking hand and pulled her over on the flat roof. Then Hans came; he made it easily too.

It was time for their mother to jump, but she didn't dare. She was paralyzed with fear. I whispered to her, "Don't look down, just take one big step."

"Mother, you can do it. It's easy," one of them called out.

"Sshh!" I hissed.

It seemed like forever before she finally made it. Then Isaak reached for me and I pulled him over, his body heavy against mine. The family embraced in relief.

"Okay," I said, "I'll tell you what we're going to do next."

"First I want to thank you, Cato. When this war is over, I hope we will see you again," Isaak panted.

"I hope so, too, but you better hurry. I'm going to jimmy the lock on somebody else's attic window. Climb through and go down the stairs, but be careful to walk close to the wall because the stairs are squeaky. You'll pass two doors on your right that belong to the people who live there. Be real quiet! Just follow the hall to the front door and that will put you on the street next to ours." I opened the window, gave them each a hug, and watched them disappear down the stairs. I just stood there, remembering the warmth of their bakery, wondering if I would ever see them again. What waited for my friends at the bottom of the stairs? What terrible thing had they done that would make someone want to kill them? I suddenly felt very cold and hurried back to my room the way I had come, over the roof.

*On the left is Cato's house, with the dorment she used to sleep on
above the window.
The flat roof on the right was where Piet and Cato stood to catch the large
aluminum cans of food the Americans dropped from their airplanes
for the Dutch people.
Cato helped her Jewish friends from the bakery escape
from the Germans by jumping from her roof to the flat roof next door.*

Not long after I helped Isaak and his family to escape over the roof, Greet's father came over one day to help Pa build a secret room in our house. Of course the Germans were forbidding us to associate with Jews, and we were scared of what might happen if the Nazis found out we were helping Jews, but as the war went on and the Germans rounded up more and more Jews, more and more people were hiding them.

Pa built the room by making a sliding partition which fit across the entrance to the small alcove where the ladder led to our attic. The room was about eight feet by ten feet, and anybody hiding there could escape up through the attic and over the roofs like Isaak and his family did. Pa was a good carpenter, and when the sliding wall was closed, nobody could tell there was a room there.

After the room was finished, Pa snuck a Jewish family into our house one night. There were five in the family, a mother and father, an aunt, and two boys. They gave Pa money he used to buy food for them off the black market. Other than creeping out very quietly to use the bathroom when we told them it was safe, they stayed in the room or sat quietly in the attic with the windows opened for ventilation. We didn't speak much to them. Pa told us to just forget they were there. People all over the city were hiding Jews, but you couldn't trust your own family not to turn you into the Germans. After seven months, Pa snuck them out again. He never did say where they went, only that they had a chance to escape.

While the Jewish family was hiding upstairs, Pa finally told us he would take us to help him steal food from farms that had been stolen by the Nazis. He told us to go to sleep and he would wake us when it was time to leave. "When I say go to sleep, I mean it, because it could take all night to steal food from those swine, and I can't take along kids who are tired," he ordered.

Afraid he might change his mind, we went straight to bed. I went upstairs to my bed in my folks' room because Pa was sober. Of course,

I was too excited to sleep and I could hear talking downstairs. I must have finally dozed off, because before long I felt Pa shaking me awake. "Cato, it's time to get ready," he whispered. In the dark I could see him holding out the black outfit Ma had made for me. "Put these on and come downstairs for instructions." I was instantly alert, eager to take on the Germans. I couldn't fight them in the streets, but I could get back at them in my own way. I hurriedly put on the black one-piece suit, tied the hood under my chin, and scurried downstairs.

As Pa rubbed soot from inside our chimney on our hands and faces as well as his own, he explained what we were to do. "You have to be careful, more so than ever," he warned us. "You cannot talk at all, not even whisper. You never know when someone is watching and you know how far a voice can carry. Stay in the shadow of a building at all times and as close as you can to any wall. When we get to a field, get down on your bellies and crawl under the barbed wire fence." He handed us each an old potato sack. He went on, "As soon as we're under the fence, we'll spread out and dig through the dirt as we crawl, looking for sugar beets, potatoes, whatever we can find."

"Do we have to split up, Pa?" I asked.

"Yes, Cato, it gives us three chances for getting food instead of just one."

And three chances of getting shot, I thought, but I kept quiet.

"When your sack gets heavy," Pa continued in his secretive voice, "come back to the fence where we split up." He was talking to us like adults to be trusted and I liked it. "If you see a food cellar near a house, stay away from it. Most likely it is guarded by a soldier with a gun or a dog.

"I hate teaching you how to steal, but the food is rightfully ours and it is better than starving to death. I hope you know that if things weren't this bad, I would never have you do this." Pa's words resounded with Dutch pride and determination.

Pa had chosen a cloudy night, with no moon or starlight and, of course, no city lights because of the blackout. I could almost feel the bricks scrape against my cheek as we crept silently next to the buildings on our street, dashing quickly across any open space to the next wall. "This is scary," Piet whispered. Pa grabbed his shoulders sternly.

"No talking at all!" he hissed.

When we finally came to a field, Pa stopped us, pointed to the ground, and we knew this was the point where we were to separate. Cautiously, quietly, I scooted under the barbed wire, squirming along in the dirt as Pa had told us to do. I was so quiet I could barely hear myself moving. In the darkness ahead I saw the low outline of one of the cellars Pa told us about. His warning echoed in my head like a gunshot. I stopped, peering around for any sign of movement. There wasn't any. I pulled myself to within a few feet of the building. Should I or shouldn't I go closer? Before I could come up with an answer, I'd jumped up and ran down the stairs light as a feather. My heartbeats were louder than my footsteps. Not until I had reached the bottom of the steps did I stop to wonder if there was a soldier watching me. Oh well, I thought, it's too late to wonder about it now.

I managed to find a latch and push open the door. It was even darker inside, but I could see shelves filled with things and I started stuffing them into my bag. My only thought was to take everything I could from the Nazis. Soon the sack was so heavy I had to stop, but as I dragged it back through the door, I froze in my tracks. A soldier stood smoking a cigarette at the top of the stairs! My muscles turned to stone; my breathing became so shallow I couldn't even hear it. Absolutely motionless, I watched the end of the cigarette get brighter every time the soldier took a drag. He turned and looked down the stairs—I could swear his eyes looked right into mine. My heart seemed to flutter and stop. He, too, stood motionless for what seemed like eternity. Then he looked away and exhaled smoke into the night air. Was it too dark to see me or did he know I was there and didn't let on?

The heavy sack began slipping through my aching fingers. Was he ever going to finish that cigarette? He took one last puff, ground the butt out with the toe of his boot, and walked away. I stood rigid, too afraid to sigh from relief. Far away I heard a door slam. He must have gone inside the farmhouse. I pulled my sack up the stairs, took a careful look around and dropped to my belly, crawling in earnest to our meeting place. Only Piet was there, afraid Pa and I had been caught.

"Do you think they caught Pa?" I whispered breathlessly.

"No," he answered softly. "If they caught him, we would have heard shouting."

A faint rustling sound caught our attention and Piet jerked his head and squinted in the direction of the farmhouse. "Somebody's coming. Duck your head. Maybe it's Pa, but maybe it's not." Pa meant life, a soldier could mean death.

It was Pa all right. "Let's go," he said quietly.

"Pa, I got. . ." I began.

"Hush, Cato. Wait til we get home," he said uneasily.

We sneaked back the way we came and found Ma worried sick. When we emptied our sacks on the kitchen floor, sugar beets, a few potatoes and carrots and lots of dirt came tumbling out of Pa's and Piet's sacks. Then I emptied mine. My folks gasped. Out of the sack came boxes, cans, bags—sugar, marmalade, butter, flour, salt.

"Did you go into a cellar?" Pa demanded angrily. "Why didn't you listen to me?"

"I watched the building real close and no one was there except a soldier smoking a cigarette when I came out," I said, almost crying. "He just walked off."

"You took an awful chance to do that, Cato," he said gruffly, but Ma smiled for the first time in months.

"Look at all this food!" Piet squealed. "It will last us for weeks."

"You did a good job, Cato," Pa admitted grudgingly. "But don't take any more chances like that."

Whether taking chances or not, fear and horror became everyday experiences as the war went on. One morning, soldiers pounded on our front door and ordered everyone to go to the park immediately, the park where I used to dangle from trees. My family joined hundreds of others who were forced to walk silently to the park and watch as sixteen men and boys were pushed into a line at gunpoint. Though their hands and legs were bound, they stood with dignity. Ma tried to cover our eyes, but I had to watch. Some of the boys didn't look any older than Piet. An SS man shouted into his megaphone that these people were to be punished for being "spies."

A woman in the crowd began crying to the soldier, pointing to the boy at the end of the line, "That is my son. He is so young yet, only fourteen years old." As she rushed forward, the officer strode toward her and, with clenched teeth, struck her across the face with his fist. She fell to the ground, weeping, begging, "Please sir, don't hurt my son. He is innocent." In a rage, the officer kicked his heavy boots into her stomach and walked away as she writhed in agony on the ground. Tears spilled down my face. Pa cursed under his breath, but we kept quiet to save ourselves from the same fate. I felt sick inside. I knew I was seeing something unspeakably evil.

Upon the orders of the officer, a line of riflemen stood at attention. Another command and the rifles were raised. "Dear God in heaven, dear God in heaven," I heard somebody groan. Behind us, a Catholic priest was hastily muttering prayers. Another command and there was a noise so loud my ears rang. The soldiers shot these people point blank in their foreheads. The "men" fell lifeless on the ground, their scarlet blood pooling under their heads. As the soldiers put their rifles down with satisfaction, we could give no sign of our helpless fury.

A garbage man was ordered to pick up the bodies with his pitchfork, load them on his cart, and take them to the garbage dump. As he began his gruesome task, the woman on the ground began to scream, "You murderers, you swine, you bastards, I will get you for this!" She raised an angry fist. "Let me take my son's body home!" She struggled to stand. The officer saw her, drew his pistol and shot her twice. My body felt numb. People all around me were crying, some from grief, some from anger. We were forced to stay and watch as the garbage man scooped up the bodies on his big pitchfork and heaved them onto his wagon. I thought I would never see a worse sight than this.

I told Greet I would never walk through the park again. For me, it was stained forever.

After one particularly heavy bombing, we emerged from our dismal cellar to a sky brighter than dawn. "Pa, look at the sky," I marveled.

"There must be a fire somewhere, Cato," he explained.

"Can Piet and I go see where it is?" I asked eagerly.

"You'd better not, Cato," he said, his face tightening with worry.

"Please, Pa, the safe siren went on."

"Oh, all right," he relented. "But hurry back and stay out of the way of the Nazis."

Piet and I ran toward the light and saw that a large hotel only a few blocks from our home was burning like crazy. A crowd of people was cheering and shouting things like, "Burn, burn in hell!" I was mad and disgusted. I asked a man dressed in his housecoat what had happened.

"I don't know how he did it," he said with awe, "but an American plane got shot down and the pilot managed to crash the plane into that hotel where the German soldiers were eating dinner." Ecstatically he gazed at the enormous fire. "When I got here, I could hear them screaming!"

A woman turned away from the searing heat and asked, "Why aren't the fire trucks here yet?"

Someone shouted, "I hope they never get here. Burn in hell, you lousy Krauts!"

Another voice rang out, "It serves them right, the lousy swine!"

We ran home to tell our folks all about the fire. I never wished any-one real harm, but I felt those soldiers deserved it for what happened to those poor people at the park. We heard that 1200 soldiers were killed. Perhaps it was an accident after all, but we considered that unknown American pilot a true hero. It was the first time I celebrated death.

It wasn't many days after that when my father told us all to sit down so he could tell us something. He was so solemn it worried me. We waited apprehensively for everyone to get settled and then announced that he had received orders to serve in the army. "But Pa, there must be a mistake!" I insisted.

"No, Cato, there is no mistake. I report next weekend. You will need to be very brave while I am gone. Piet, I want you to take care of your mother and sister—you know what a hothead she can be. You're the oldest in the family now and I'm depending on you to handle any situation that comes up."

Piet looked at Pa with fear-filled eyes, barely able to choke out the words, "I will, Pa." It was a big order for a boy of twelve.

Pa looked sternly at me. "Cato, I want you to be double careful."

"What for, Pa? I can handle those lousy Nazis."

"I know you think you can handle them, but they can handle you, too. Don't ever take chances with them. Don't trust any of them. Don't speak back to them, and try to be polite," he instructed me.

"But Pa, I hate them. They're killers, just like you always told us," I insisted.

"You can hate them, but don't take any chances, especially when you and Piet go out to find food."

I thought for awhile and could see he was right.

"I won't," I sighed.

Pa's voice grew even fiercer. "If you ever become members of the Nazi party, no matter where I am, I will come back and I will kill my own kids!" He spoke with such intensity I knew he would do it.

On the day Pa had to go away, hundreds and hundreds of old men and young boys crowded into the train station. The young ones didn't look much older than Piet; the older ones were dressed in uniforms from the World War twenty-five years before, many of them too small. Children and wives hung on the men as they exchanged final good-byes, crying, whispering, afraid their secrets might be the last they would ever share. As Pa bent down to say good-bye, my tears almost washed away the loathing I had felt for him. My concern for him felt new and uncomfortable. I told him, "Pa, don't worry about Ma and Piet. I'll take good care of them." My father just smiled sadly. A Nazi marched toward him and ordered him to move along.

"I have to go now. Be careful and don't trust anyone," were the last words I would hear Pa speak for a long, long time. It was the only time in my life I saw Pa hug Ma. And for the first time ever, I could feel a kind of love for my father flowing through me. Tears ran down my face freely as I cried, "Good-bye, Pa, take care." Ma and Piet were crying and calling to him, too. The German soldiers packed the train cars so tightly I wondered if Pa would be able to breathe. Hundreds of Dutchmen hung from the windows waving to their families, but I couldn't see Pa. As a band played the first notes of the Dutch national anthem, everyone became very quiet. German soldiers kept walking up and down the platform yelling, "Heil Hitler, Heil Hitler!" No one responded. Then the Nazis started brutally kicking some old people so a few people began echoing faintly, "Heil Hitler." I raised my hand, too, but as soon as no one was looking, I made a slicing motion across my throat with my hand, especially when I said Hitler's name.

We couldn't even take the streetcar home that day because the Krauts had stolen almost all of them.

CHAPTER THIRTEEN

*For some—Jews, Gypsies, blacks and most Slavs—there
was no place in [the Nazis'] new world order. For those
who did not wish to serve the Master Race, who wished to
be free to live their own lives, to think their own thoughts,
there was no place. They too would be eliminated.*

INA R. FRIEDMAN, *THE OTHER VICTIMS*

Who could have guessed that an innocent conversation with Greet
would be the first link in the chain of events that led me to the concentration camp at Nordhausen. Walking along the canal one rainy
afternoon, I said, "Hey, let's go see Henny and Jenny. I haven't seen
them for a long time."

"My folks don't want me inside a Nazi's house," Greet shuddered.

"Mine either, but I'm curious. Let's just go for the heck of it," I
pressed her.

"Oh, all right, but I can't stay long," she conceded.

When their father opened the door, the sight of his black SS uniform made me sick. He smiled at us and asked us why he hadn't seen us
for such a long time. I was tempted to tell him it was because he was a
traitor to Holland, but I held my tongue. He sent us upstairs to the
twins' room, where a boy in a Hitler Youth uniform was sitting with
them. He immediately jumped up, stiffened, and gave the Heil Hitler
salute. I muttered under my breath, "Go to hell," but I raised my arm
halfheartedly and mumbled the words. So did Greet. We feared a beating if we didn't. Henny asked, "Cato, Greet, how are you?"

"Oh, fine, I guess," I answered.

"You say you are fine, but you both look so skinny," Henny blurted out.

"Whose fault is that?" I snapped. "Those lousy Krauts steal all our food and let everyone starve to death."

Jenny broke in, "Don't say that about the Germans. They are good people. If you're hungry, join our party and you'll have enough to eat."

"I'd rather eat rabbit shit," I said.

"Don't talk that way. You and Greet should come with us sometime and see what it is really like," Jenny argued. "I think there is a party next week with lots of good food."

"Yes," Henny chimed in. "Come with us. When is it, Hans?"

The boy answered, "I think it is next Tuesday night and we can invite anyone we want."

Greet looked skeptical. "Cato, I better go home now."

I had underestimated the revulsion I felt for my former friends, Henny and Jenny, and I wanted to go home, too. As we turned to leave, Henny said cheerfully, "Even if Greet can't come, you can bring your brother."

"I'd rather steal the food back from those swine who stole it from us in the first place," I shot back. "C'mon, Greet, let's go."

Once we were out their front door, Greet whispered, "Cato, I have a funny feeling about this party of theirs. I don't trust them, do you?"

"Not a bit. But a plate of food sure sounds good to me right now. Especially food that isn't out of someone's garbage can. Have you ever eaten dog meat, Greet?"

"I think so," she said and shuddered again.

"Well, we had some last week, and it sure must have been an old dog, because all of us came down with bad cramps that night."

"Maybe someone tried to poison it, do you think?" she asked.

"Who knows? But if I had known for sure, I would have invited some Germans over for dinner!"

I told Greet how skinny and weak Mollie was getting. "Why didn't you have your Pa kill her before he left, Cato? That way she wouldn't have to suffer any longer," Greet said.

"I could never do that, Greet," I gasped. "Mollie is the only one I have in this world who really loves me." Knowing my folks, she didn't try to argue with me.

Later that week, we were in one of the city's squares when we saw a German soldier beating two small Jewish children with the butt of his rifle. People stared or walked by without looking. Greet tugged at my sleeve, "Cato, look what that soldier is doing to those kids. Shouldn't we do something?"

"We better not," I said, though I couldn't turn away. "He'll do the same thing to us." Why was I so small and weak? Hatred laced with helplessness created a rage I could hardly contain. But out of fear for my own life, I, too, turned away.

Another time, the Nazis had hanged five Jews in the square and left a soldier to guard them—as if those corpses could walk away. The sight turned our stomachs. A sign identified the dead men as Jews and forbade anyone from cutting their bloated bodies down. The families of these husbands and sons were forced to let them hang there until the bodies were rotting away. "What is this thing the Nazis have with the Jews?" I asked Greet. "Those soldiers aren't even human beings anymore. They're nothing but animals."

"I don't want to insult the animals of this world by calling Nazis animals. I don't understand it, either. Let's get out of here. I can't stand it anymore." On the way home, we heard the braying jackass horns of the trucks moving through the streets rounding up Jews again. I wondered if Isaak was safe somewhere or dangling lifeless from a Nazi's rope.

There is just no way to escape all this, I thought bitterly. I was watching life slip away from my friends and me. Henny and Jenny were Hitler Youth, and Greet and I were starving. We weren't teaching Sonja to walk anymore because she was too weak from hunger to stand on her feet.

"Let's go look for some food, Greet," I suggested.

"I don't know," she answered halfheartedly, "It's getting harder and harder to find anything and there seem to be more guards on the streets. I'm hungry all the time, but I think they're wise to what people are doing."

"What else can we do? You look awful; your arms and legs are as skinny as bones and your stomach is pouched out in front of you."

"You don't have to tell me, Cato. You look lousy, too, okay?" she grumbled. Hunger was eating away at our sympathy for each other.

Between all the hunger and misery, we could still think of ways to have fun. We had eaten most of the food the planes had dropped and had stored the empty cans in the corner of our yard. With our collection and some from the neighbors, we were sure we had enough cans to make a dandy boat. So we went to work. First we drilled tiny holes in each corner of the square cans, then put the lids back on. We wired four abreast for the wide part of the boat, then three across, narrowing to one at the tip. We took an old strip of metal and wrapped it all the way around the boat, added a broomstick and an old sheet for a sail, and headed for the canal. We had quite a group of people following us; even some soldiers stopped to chuckle and tease us. We didn't care. Piet and I pounded huge nails in the poles that held up the bridge, so we could climb down when we wanted to go sailing. We liked to take the lids off a few cans and fill them with muddy water that we could soak our feet in as we sailed. Even in the rain, we spent hours on the water, up and down Amsterdam's many canals, trying to lose ourselves in fantasy, pretending life still had hope.

But the hunger was inescapable. It began to feel like a spoon scraping against my insides. Piet and I still stood in line for hours for a tiny pan of watery cabbage soup from the emergency kitchen set up at our school, but it didn't touch the emptiness. Finally Henny and Jenny invited us to another Hitler Youth party and I couldn't resist. Greet was adamant about not going, so I worked on Piet. "Hey, Piet," I teased, "are you hungry?"

"Don't be stupid, Cato. Of course I'm hungry," he snapped.

*A drawing of the boat Cato and Piet built out of cans
from the American food drop.*

"Well, how would you like to go to a party with me tonight and fill your belly with all the good food you want? Henny and Jenny invited me to one of their parties and said I could bring you!" I said eagerly.

"Are you sure it's safe to go? We don't belong to Hitler Youth," he said with disgust. He didn't want to betray Pa.

"Of course, it's safe. Their folks are going, too. They said they are inviting lots of kids. Maybe we can bring some food home for Ma," I reassured him.

"Where is Ma? We can't go without telling her," Piet said. Since Pa had left, she had kept us almost tied to the house, but that day I had not seen her. The Hitler Youth party started at five o'clock, and it was already past four.

"You get changed into some decent clothes and I'll write her a note. Hurry!" I urged him. I made Piet put on some pants with two pockets on the side with another in the back and I chose a dress with four pockets sewn on the front. I think Ma had sewn on the pockets for just such an occasion. As we shut the front door we saw Henny and Jenny walking toward our house in their blue and white uniforms, with their folks right behind them. It was August 4, 1943.

"Hi, Cato," Henny smiled. "Are you ready?"

"Yes, we are. Do we look okay? And is it still all right with your folks if we come?" I asked.

Jenny answered, "It's fine with them, but they said it would be good if you two don't talk tonight."

"Well, why not?" I asked suspiciously.

"Because you don't speak German like we do. Just pretend that you are our cousins and that you are deaf and dumb, okay?"

That sounded strange, but I thought at least we wouldn't have to talk to any of the Nazis or shout "Heil Hitler." I don't know why, but I didn't want to let them know that I had learned to understand and speak German.

"Okay, sure. You can do that, can't you, Piet?" I asked. He shrugged in agreement.

In a few short minutes, we were at a brightly lit hotel. At the sight of so many German trucks and soldiers, I almost turned around and ran home. But I could already smell the aroma of fresh bread, and memories of Hans and Jopie flooded over me. I wasn't even inside and my mouth was watering, my legs weak. As we climbed the red-carpeted stairs toward the big double doors, the twins gave the "Heil Hitler" greeting, but I just looked down at the ground. I had resolved to never salute Adolf Hitler again. In a large banquet room, I saw hundreds of German soldiers laughing, drinking from huge steins of beer, standing by long tables loaded with food. Enormous red-and-black swastikas lined the walls. What was I doing here with these traitors, I thought with revulsion. If my stomach hadn't been so empty, I would have thrown up.

There was more food than I had ever seen assembled in one place—rolls, apples, oranges, potatoes, beef roasts, hams, turkeys, pastries, and pies—all the things we thought we would never taste again. Henny and Jenny found us a place to sit down at a banquet table. We were surrounded by kids. Young waitresses in black dresses and little white aprons brought around plates piled with food. Those of us not in uniform were interspersed with those who were, like bedraggled weeds trying to survive in a well-ordered garden. We were so skinny next to them. As soon as Piet and I were served, the world beyond my plate might as well have disappeared. Gravy dripped down our chins as we ate as though this were our last meal. Gulping down the food, I was struck by the realization that just outside this hotel door, thousands of families would not be able to sleep tonight because of their hunger. Our stomachs were so shrunken that minutes after starting to devour the food, we were bursting! I was furious to think of all this plenty for the Germans when we had nothing.

Henny and Jenny abruptly got up to go look for their folks, telling Piet and I to wait at the table. Piet and I sat at the table until it seemed they had been gone for an awfully long time. "Piet," I whispered, "where are they?"

"I don't know," he answered, his eyes searching the corners of the hall for the twins. Almost everybody had gone. "Where did all the other kids go?"

They must have slipped out while we were stuffing ourselves. Except for the waitresses scraping leftover food into a big garbage can, we were alone in the room. I dug my fingers into Piet's arm and murmured,

"Something's wrong. I can feel it, can't you?"

"Yes," he hissed, "let's go home, Cato!" He pulled me to my feet and we made our way through the tables and chairs toward the door.

Piet suddenly stopped. "What about Ma?" he asked. "We better go over and get some food for Ma." I didn't argue. We turned in unison and headed for the table still loaded with food. As we walked swiftly by the table, our hands flew from plate to pocket and back again as we stuffed in every roll, potato, or piece of meat we could until our clothes were bulging. Then we raced for the door, hurrying down the hall and into the night air. We knew it was getting too close to curfew time to be out on the streets.

As soon as we got outside, we saw Henny and Jenny standing next to one of the trucks talking with a German officer. We could hear the strange muffled sound of children crying, but we couldn't tell where it was coming from. "Henny, Jenny, over here!" I yelled. Henny pointed at us, and the officer raised his hand and snapped his fingers at two other soldiers and then he pointed at us, too. The two Nazis took a step toward us.

"Let's get the hell out of here," I shouted at Piet. "Run, just run. I'll see you at home." I bolted for freedom with every bit of determination my weak body could muster, but the two soldiers caught us and wrestled us to the ground. I cried out from pain as one of them twisted my arm and roughly searched me up and down. I could understand their German perfectly as one held my rolls aloft like a trophy and shouted, "We have found two more who have stolen food from their providers. Into the truck with them!" I felt caught in the iron jaws of a trap, as if my bones were snapping under the force of the soldiers' hands. One guard held up a canvas flap as the other tossed us like trash into the back of a truck already teeming with sobbing children. Most of the children were much smaller than Piet and I.

Where were Henny and Jenny? I wanted to get to the back of the truck so I could jump out, but I felt tangled in the squirming arms and legs of the other children. The soldiers dropped a green tarpaulin across the back and plunged us into darkness. The truck lurched forward, knocking me down.

We began our descent into hell.

I pulled my arms and legs up tightly, trying not to touch anyone. As my eyes grew accustomed to the darkness, I could see a small, weeping girl and pulled her onto my lap. She was calling for her parents. I could see other older children holding younger ones, smoothing their hair, trying to quiet them. A soldier shouted for us to be silent, kicking the children nearest him. He sat down at the back of the truck with a rifle between his knees. Howls quieted to whimpers and sniffles that could be choked back but not silenced on command. We slipped into shock.

"I'm sorry. I should have listened to Greet," I whispered to Piet. My tears came in waves I couldn't stop, but I tried not to make a sound. "I want to go home," I cried as softly as I could. Piet put his arm around my shoulder, trying to be the big brother he was, but it didn't help.

"I'm going to kill Henny and Jenny when I get back," I hissed.

"Oh, you don't mean that," Piet said in a low voice, trying to avoid the guard's wrath.

"I sure do mean it. Do you think they're taking us to one of their camps they brag so much about?" I asked in sudden panic.

"I don't think so, Cato. I heard that only the Jews are being sent there. They know we aren't Jews. Let's just wait and see what happens." Then we settled into a tense silence.

CHAPTER FOURTEEN

The Nazis took my mother far away from me, to a place
[from] which people cannot come back. Nine years old, I
learned then a never-ceasing deep sorrow. Even now,
Mother's Day is the saddest day of the year for me.

MARTHA HEINZ

Before long, the truck stopped, the tarp was pulled back, and the soldiers jumped down and pointed their rifles at us. *"Raus! Raus!"* (Out! Out!) they shouted. What big bullies they are, I thought, standing there holding their guns over a bunch of kids. It showed me what cowards they really were. We jumped or fell from the truck and were herded into a flat-bottomed boat floating by a dock. If any of the kids stumbled or tripped, a guard kicked them back into line.

I couldn't tell where we were. There must have been at least 300 of us ordered to climb down a ladder and get into the hull of the boat. Dazed and disoriented, we clung to each other and did as we were told. One of the soldiers said bitingly, "All of you have stolen something from your providers. All of you will be punished."

I yelled out in German, "I hate you, you swine. You've stolen us from our parents." He could have beaten me for speaking out, but he ignored me.

He continued, "You will be going to a special camp, a work camp. You must work hard to pay for your crimes against the German people."

We tumbled down the ladder, always hurried by the rifles against our legs, our feet crushing the tiny fingers of those below us. A guard followed us down, carrying a barrel and shouting, *"Achtung! Achtung!"*

(Attention! Attention!) He told us to use the barrel to do our business in and if we got seasick, use it for that, too.

As he turned to go, a young boy called out, "But what about our parents?" The guard quickly stepped over to him and slapped him hard across the face, sending him sprawling against the kids behind him. The boy jumped back up, shouting, "You German pig. Don't you ever . . ." Blows from the guard's stick landed on the boy's head, and he crumpled to the floor. Even then, the guard hit him again and again. When I had taunted a guard, had I escaped such a brutal beating because I was a girl? I'd better watch my mouth, I thought. I might not be so lucky next time.

The guard laughed the meanest laugh I had ever heard and slapped the stick he carried against his leg as he turned sharply. He hung up a small oil lantern, climbed back up the ladder, and closed the top of our prison. Again darkness encircled us, except for the dim light of the lantern. Our crying echoed off the coffinlike walls.

All I wanted to do was sleep, but the events of the night kept running through my mind. I could not believe what my friends had done to us. I remembered Pa warning, "Never trust anyone; be extra careful." If only I had listened, but how could I have known? How did Greet know?

We could hear airplanes overhead and the sound of bombs exploding somewhere in the water. With each explosion, we cowered and ducked, though it wouldn't have done us any good. I felt the boat bump against the boat pulling us. The Germans must all be on that boat, I thought, so they won't have to listen to us cry. When we began rocking back and forth, I knew we were going out to sea. It was so crowded, we just did the best we could by taking the smaller kids on our laps. We tried to comfort the littlest ones, even though we were frantic ourselves, with no idea where we were going. The dim light from the lantern fell on the cheek of the girl next to Piet and me. She looked about my age. "What's your name?" I asked.

"Rosie. What's yours?"

"Cato, and this is my brother, Piet."

"Were you at the party too? You look like a Jew," Piet blurted out.

"Yes, I am. I went to the party because I heard some people talking about the free food."

"Well, my so-called friends invited us. My folks don't even know where we are."

"I don't know where my folks are," she said sadly. "They were picked up a year ago by the Germans and I haven't heard from them. Maybe they are dead." Rosie's voice seemed ancient and wise.

"How old are you, Rosie?" I asked.

"Eleven."

My questions tumbled out. "What have you been doing since your folks left? Where have you been staying? How come they didn't pick you up with your parents?"

"They didn't pick me up because I was at my friend's house," she explained. "When I got home, there were so many people in my house taking our furniture and breaking the windows that I got scared and hid behind a fence until they left. I didn't dare go back inside my house for fear the soldiers were still there."

"So you have been living on the streets all alone?" asked Piet in amazement.

"Where else could I go? I have been hiding in bomb shelters whenever I see a soldier."

"What about food?" I asked.

"I went hungry most of the time, but sometimes I stole from the Germans' prostitutes. I went through their garbage," she explained shamelessly.

"We did, too," I admitted. At that moment I knew I wanted Rosie to stay by my side, to be my friend through whatever peril we would face.

With no fresh air, the odor quickly became unbearable. The rocking motion was making kids throw up everywhere. We were packed in so tightly, we couldn't even sit comfortably, let alone make it to the barrel. Then diarrhea hit. Kids had to let themselves go where they were. I gasped for breath only when I absolutely had to; I could almost taste the stench. Just then, someone lifted the "lid" of our prison and two soldiers came down with a bucket of watery cabbage soup and a single bowl. No bread. One soldier dipped the bowl into the soup, gave it to the nearest child, waited, then scooped up some in the same bowl for the next child. Those with any strength pushed forward for their share first. I sat and waited with distaste for my turn. The soldiers escaped the terrible smell as quickly as they could. Then it seemed that everyone was retching. We were swimming in our own waste. As the hours passed, my skin felt as though it were being eaten away.

Talking with Rosie helped me fight the terrible fear gnawing at me. She told me she never expected to see her mother and father again and how much she loved them. Thoughts of Pa filled me with a peculiar longing for him. And Ma, was she frantic with worry? Rosie talked of her parents with dry eyes. I guess she had no tears left inside her. I thought maybe I would be the same someday, with no tears left to cry.

"I wonder which camp they are going to send us to," I said to Rosie. "Maybe we will go where your folks are."

"It doesn't matter," she answered grimly. "They said they kill all the Jews."

"Well, I'm not a Jew. Why would they want to kill me?" I stopped myself abruptly when the dark truth hit me. The Nazis did not need a reason to kill anyone. Rosie was Jewish, I was not. She didn't deserve to die any more than I did merely because of the family she was born to. I knew that anyone who could kill a creature as gentle as Rosie would kill me without hesitation.

As I felt the protection of my non-Jewishness slip away, an awareness began growing in me that I could not express until many years later. It was the realization that hatred is a poison of such corrosive strength that it cannot be contained. I was not a Jew. I was one small Dutch girl caught in the hatred aimed at someone else. I did not know who else the acid of hate would find. The racial line between Rosie and me disappeared, and I knew then that I must take her Jewish hand in mine and stand as her friend against whatever was to come.

It was the next night when food came again, the same watery soup, except this time it was very cold. I didn't eat because I didn't want to get sick again. The children were mostly still, as if they were just waiting to see what would happen to them. I had found a small dark-haired boy about five years old to hold and care for. He seemed to be without a brother or a friend and cried pitifully for his mother. He was frightfully thin, as fragile as a petal in the wind. He was so light I barely knew he was there. It had felt good to cradle him in my lap and feel his arm on mine as his rigid fear softened into sleep. I, too, slept.

When I woke, he was still asleep and I wondered who he was and who loved and was searching for him. I put my hand on his back wishing I could shield him from any more pain when I noticed that he was too still. I couldn't feel the faint in and out of his breathing that had soothed me to sleep.

"Piet! Piet!" I called softly into the darkness. "Come here and look at this little boy."

Piet must have been awake already because he quickly leaned over and touched the boy. In a minute, he whispered, "Cato, he's dead."

The weight of Piet's words was unbearable. How could he be dead? I became terribly frightened that somehow his death would spread to me and tried to push him off my lap. "Piet, get him away from me," I cried hysterically.

Piet took him from my arms. "Cato," he said sternly, "don't carry on so much. He's not suffering anymore. I have the feeling that before we get back home we are going to see a lot of dead people. They can't hurt you, Cato." My brother sounded like an old man to me. We placed the boy gently between us in some straw, and I saw he still had his thumb in his mouth.

Anger rose in me as strong as if I had seen him crushed beneath the boots of the Nazi guards. I ran my finger across his cheek, curled up by him, and waited for morning. I had never even asked him his name. I felt so old.

When the soldiers came down, I pointed out the boy and watched as they carried him and several other tiny bodies up the ladder. "What are they going to do with the bodies?" I asked Piet.

"Probably throw them into the ocean," Piet answered bitterly.

We were on the boat for two days and three nights. Once a day a soldier or two, always with handkerchiefs tied over their noses, would come down to empty the barrel, pick up the bodies, and give us soup. I hoped they would fall down and break their necks or catch a disease from one of the dead children they had to carry up the ladder. Children cried off and on, some having convulsions, others sick all the time. We couldn't move without touching excrement or vomit. Talking with Rosie and Piet was the only thing that took my mind off it. We talked for hours about what we would do if we got out of there alive. We desperately wanted to survive and tell someone what they had done to us. I remember saying, "I don't think it can get any worse."

"Don't count on it, Cato," Piet said glumly. "It could get lots worse."

"Let's make an oath then that if one of us gets back alive, we will hunt down the scum who got us here in the first place and make sure they get punished," I said. All three of us swore on it.

When the boat landed, we got out in an industrial area of a city. We looked like a bunch of filthy rags and smelled like we had not had a bath in months. We were starving and weary from lack of sleep. Many of the children made pitiful cries, like newborn animals. Our German captors yelled, *"Raus! Raus!* Be quick about it. Line up in rows of five and stand at attention!" If we weren't quick enough on the ladder or we stumbled, a soldier would yank our arms and shove us into a row.

Rosie took my arm. "Let's all three of us stay together, okay? Maybe we can help each other," she said.

"No matter where they take us, I'm going to get out," I declared.

"Shh!" said Rosie. "You better be quiet or they'll beat you up."

"I don't care if they hear me, and if I get my hands on one of those twins, I'm going to kill her." Rosie stared straight ahead and said nothing.

When we got all lined up in rows of five to the guards' satisfaction, I could tell there weren't nearly as many children as there had been on the trucks. More than half seemed to be missing. Dead and tossed into the sea, I supposed. We saw a large building in front of us with a sign that said it was a cheese factory. "I bet they don't make any cheese in there now," I whispered to Rosie.

"Shh! They might hear you."

I wondered where Henny and Jenny were. I wondered if Greet would still try to help Sonja walk. Just thinking about my two good friends made me cry, and thinking about the twins made me spit in the dirt, which there was plenty of.

Only about a third of us survived the ordeal on the boat. The soldiers marched those of us who were left into the factory. We could smell the most delicious aroma of food. Inside were long wooden tables like the ones at the party so long ago. Had it been only three days? We were ordered to sit down and someone handed me a plate loaded with food. After a few wonderful gulps, we heard a piercing siren and the drone of airplanes. The Germans yelled in panicky voices, *"Raus! Raus!"* We grabbed our plates, trying to shovel food into our mouths while we ran to a nearby shelter. We knew no one could outrun a bomb, but we all tried. Explosions close by spurred us on faster and faster. Suddenly I felt a sharp pain in my right leg and looked down to a stream of blood pouring from just above my ankle.

"Piet! Rosie! Stop!" I screamed. "I'm hit. Help me, help me." I fell to the ground with blood running through my fingers where I had grabbed my leg. Food lay scattered on the ground around me. Rosie ran toward me and knelt down, tears making tracks down her dirty face. The fierce burning in my leg sent me into spasms of crying.

Piet ran to me, moaning, "Cato, you're hurt!"

"I can see that, Piet," I said sarcastically. I felt like I was going to faint.

"Let's get into the shelter. Maybe there will be someone who can help you," Rosie said. She was so calm, as if she had been through this many times before.

"Just don't bring a lousy swine soldier to me," I spat. "Can't you and Piet get it out? And hurry, it hurts like hell."

"Don't cuss, Cato," Rosie said. "It isn't going to help a bit."

"How would you know?" I said bitterly. "You didn't get hit. I did."

Holding me between them, they dragged me into the shelter. We sat down on a bench and Rosie ripped off a piece of her slip to use as a bandage. "Hold her down," she said to Piet. "I can see the shrapnel in her leg, and I'm going to pull it out."

She tied the strip of fabric above the wound. "This will stop the bleeding," she explained. "Now take hold of your brother's hand and squeeze real hard."

"Is it going to hurt bad?" I groaned.

"Yes," she said firmly, "but don't scream too loud or those soldiers will come over and you never know what they might do." While I gripped Piet's hands, Rosie probed with her fingers inside the open wound. Tears filled my eyes from the searing pain, but not a sound escaped my lips. Rosie pulled out a piece of ragged metal and as she went in for more, the pain became so unbearable I let out a shriek. A man with a small black bag came running over to me.

He knelt down next to me and opened his bag as he said, "You're hurt. I'm a doctor. Let me have a look."

I took one look at his SS uniform and snarled, "No lousy Kraut is going to touch me. Get away from me!" I took aim and landed a hard kick in his groin, right where it hurt, and knocked him backward onto the dirt floor of the shelter. He jumped back up red in the face and madder than anything. Without a word, he shut his bag and snapped his fingers at two soldiers who had been watching. After he said something to them in a low voice they yanked me to my feet and started beating me with their rifles and kicking me with their boots.

Piet and Rosie pulled on their arms, begging them to stop, but they stopped only when they heard the doctor telling them to. I could taste salty blood running into my mouth, but I was so mad I turned my face away so the soldiers could not see my tears. White from fright, Piet and Rosie helped me sit back down on the bench and pleaded with me to keep my mouth shut from now on and to watch my Dutch temper. Rosie re-tied the piece of her slip tightly around my bleeding leg. The all-clear sirens came on and Rosie and Piet helped me go outside. My whole body throbbed with pain. I knew I would be black and blue the next day, but I wouldn't give any German the satisfaction of knowing I was hurt. I vowed that no German would ever see me cry again. And I promised myself that I would never forget what they did to me that day.

CHAPTER FIFTEEN

I have told you this story not to weaken you, but to strengthen you. Now it is up to you.

PRISONER IN SACHSENHAUSEN

Outside the shelter, soldiers barked for everyone to walk in rows of five to the train depot a little way down the road. From the platform we could hear a train whistle in the distance. Soon a locomotive pulled a line of boxcars into sight, some of them open with heads and arms sticking out. It didn't look like there would be enough room for us to get on, but as the train stopped, soldiers began tossing corpses like sandbags out of the cars. Then we were ordered to get on. We were packed so tightly we couldn't sit down. Rosie and I stood on something that felt soft and discovered to our horror that it was a man's body. As the train picked up speed, we were jerked from side to side and pressed hard between people. Little ones died fast—they couldn't get any air and some were trampled when they fell. Standing on that body raised Rosie and I up high enough to breathe and probably saved our lives.

My mind couldn't grasp what I was witnessing. The clicking noises of the track, the throbbing pain where Rosie had pulled out the shrapnel, the crushing pressure of bodies against mine made tears slide down my face, but there was no one to wipe them away. Maybe I am hallucinating, I thought, from losing so much blood. Dying right then seemed like a decent alternative, but the thought of those two girls back home not having to face my wrath was enough to make me perk up and quit feeling sorry for myself. I was determined I would survive to visit my two "friends" one more time.

The train slowed. I don't know how long we had been standing there, but the sun had gone down and our throats were parched. When our boxcar was opened, we were ordered to get out. My leg was so sore and stiff that Piet and Rosie had to help me walk. Their faces looked tired and drawn. More dead were being thrown off the train and left wherever they landed for animals to devour. Rosie, Piet, and I managed to stay together as we marched with the others through the gates of hell. Walking skeletons stood inside the long fences of barbed wire. They looked like death had come for them, left its mark, and then forgotten to take them. Corpses were piled like sticks along one side of an open space. The stench was unbearable.

"What's that smell?" Piet asked. "Something is burning." The answer to his question would be given to us that night.

There was nowhere to run. Uniformed guards with distant faces were everywhere. Many had huge German shepherd dogs that bared teeth as deadly as the barbed wire on the fences at anyone who ventured too close. With their free hands, the guards threatened us with whips.

Guards shouted at us to take off our clothes and throw them into a pile. Our hesitation was met with quick snaps of whips in the air. Reluctantly pulling my dress over my head, I was flooded with the humiliation of revealing my body to strangers. With downcast eyes, we stood naked in front of each other, trying to hide our private parts from the callous stares of the Gestapo. We were told later that the clothes would be sent to German people somewhere.

As each of us was pushed forward in front of some kind of inspector, we were sent to the left or right at the flick of his wrist, having no idea what it meant. We were to find out very soon. I was sent to the right to join a long line standing by a low building. A gruff looking woman guard came by and shaved the hair off every part of our bodies. Her dull razor caught the sores under my hair, shooting pain through my head. Prisoners told us later the hair was used for stuffing pillows and mattresses. Other guards tossed black-and-white-striped prison uniforms at us and we hurriedly covered our nakedness with the ill-fitting pants and jackets. Then they ordered us into the barracks. I learned later that these barracks guards were *Sunderkommandos,* Jewish prisoners who had been forced under threat of torture to become guards. As soon as the Nazis had no use for them they were killed and replaced by others.

Children with sunken cheeks and hollow eyes stared at us as a guard led us into the crude barracks. We were each handed a thin blanket. Rough wooden slats were nailed to the walls for beds. After days of terror, starvation, heartbreak, and searing pain, I felt numbness settle over me. I was only twelve years old, and my whole life should have been before me. Instead I stared into purgatory.

The sound of a boy's voice broke through my stupor as he walked

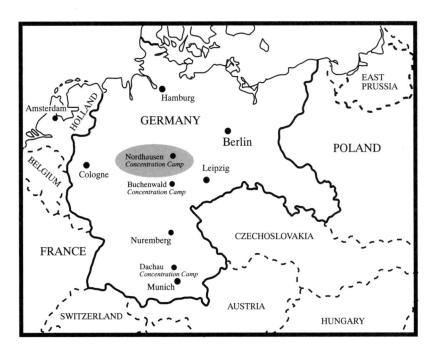

Nordhausen was only one of hundreds of concentration camps throughout Europe.

toward us. I looked up and saw the most beautiful sad eyes in a handsome face. As young as I was, my heart thumped an extra beat. The tall young man with dark curly hair told us his name was Martin. "I know how you must feel," he said wearily in German. "I went through the same thing a year ago. I thought my life was over."

Martin sat down on the dirt floor and we gathered around him, telling him our names and about the party, the boat, the cruelty. He was different from the others, the hollow ones. There was still life in his face.

"I know all about the Hitler Youth," he shuddered. "They are the meanest bunch in the world. Some of them are meaner than the Gestapo."

"You've been here a year?" someone asked. "How have you stood it so long?"

"You do whatever they order you to do and take it one day at a time," he answered. "You eat whatever they give you no matter what it tastes like."

"Why haven't you tried to escape?" I asked.

"It's impossible. The Gestapo have dogs that are trained to kill on command. The people who try to escape are torn to pieces. The only way to escape is death."

"I don't want to stay here," I wailed. "All I did was take some food the Nazis stole from us in the first place."

"I know. The Germans punish everyone who does anything they decide is wrong."

"Well, I'm not going to die in this place," I said with determination.

"We all say the same thing, Cato," Martin said solemnly.

"Are you a Jew?" Rosie asked.

"I'm only part Jew. My mother was a Jew, but both my parents were killed by the Germans."

"They killed my parents, too." Rosie's voice trembled. "I've been living on the streets for a year stealing food to survive."

"Well, you have to fight here to stay alive, too, and it's going to be lots harder than what you went through on the streets. You're lucky,

Rosie, they haven't sent you away to the showers yet."

"What is so bad about the showers?" Piet asked.

"It's not water that comes out of the spigots," Martin said in a low, somber voice. "It's gas. They kill the Jews who aren't strong enough to work. Then the bodies are tossed into ovens to be burned." In spite of the atrocities I had already seen, his words stunned me.

We listened to everything Martin told us about life in the camp, sensing that his information could mean the difference between life and death. "They won't give you enough to eat. But we can help each other."

"How?" a weak voice asked.

"When we have daily roll call, pinch each others' cheeks, so that you look healthy. Never, never let a German see that you are too tired to work. Because as soon as they find out you can't be of any use to them, you'll end up in the showers. The Germans will use you until you drop dead.

"You will probably be sent to the factory where I work," he went on. "We have to sort through all the clothes people take off when they get here and separate them into different sizes. But before you throw anything in a pile, try to feel around the hems for something hard." I kept looking back over my shoulder for guards, not wanting to be surprised by a boot against my back, but they had left us alone in our misery. Martin continued, "People think they can hide their jewelry and watches from the Germans if they sew them into their clothes."

Piet interrupted, "What do we do if we find something?"

Martin explained, "Germans are afraid of catching any sickness, so you pretend you have to puke and duck under the sorting table. While you make the sounds of throwing up, rip open the hem and take out the jewelry. I've even found diamonds and rubies."

"But what do we do with them?" I pressed.

"You stuff it on your body someplace you think it will be safe."

"What if they search you when you leave?" someone asked. I remembered the rough, probing hands of the guards outside the party.

"Sometimes they do and sometimes they don't," he said. "But you girls can hide them in a good spot. It is harder for boys."

"You mean . . . you mean . . . ?" I stuttered because I had never heard of this before and it made me feel embarrassed. No one could see me blush in the shadows, but Martin sensed my self-consciousness.

"You'll get used to it," he said with resignation. "You're going to lose all feelings of being ashamed, I can guarantee. You will do anything to survive."

"But what can we do with jewelry?" Piet asked.

"You'll find out," Martin assured him. "You can use it to bribe the guards if you need to see one of your friends in another area of the camp. Most likely they are going to separate you three. You, because you are a Jew," he pointed to Rosie, "and him because he is older," he nodded at Piet. "They'll probably make him dig ditches for the dead Jews. They use stronger kids to help throw the bodies in."

Piet gasped. "I'll never do that!"

"If you don't do it, they'll give you a bullet in the back of the head and you'll be in one of the holes. It won't make any difference to the Nazis if there is one more person in a hole than they planned."

I didn't want to hear any more. Why was Martin telling us these horrible things? I wanted to scream at him to stop. And yet Martin's description of the brutal realities that would shape my life for the next twenty months had left me with a few fragile strands of hope—try to look healthy, smuggle out some jewels, and don't ask questions. How green we were in the beginning, but how fast we caught on just to stay alive.

As I climbed up to my bunk in the dim light cast by one bare bulb, Martin saw the blood on my prison trousers. "What happened to your leg, Cato?" he asked. I pulled up my pants and he saw the bandage made of Rosie's slip, now stiff with dried blood.

"She got hit with some shrapnel from a bomb after we got off the boat," Rosie said. "I got two big pieces out, but there's more in there. It's been bleeding a lot."

"I want to be a doctor when I get out of here," Martin said, kneeling down to get a closer look. "Let me check it."

I sat down on the dirt and he gently untied the strip of cloth around my crusted wound. His tenderness kept me from crying out in anguish. He studied my leg silently a few minutes and then looked up. "I can't take out the rest of the shrapnel without some instruments. And even if I had instruments, I don't have any way to sterilize them. You're better off leaving it alone."

I spent my first night with five others in a bed that looked big enough for one, grateful to be squeezed in so we could share our body warmth. The wooden slats felt much harder than the church bench I had slept on, and I was afraid of getting slivers. I had been the "tough" one so many times in my life, the one who had to be strong. Having Martin to lean on was almost like having Derk back. Martin had helped many others, I was sure, and I felt he was truly our friend. I fell asleep remembering my faraway brother.

The next morning, everything was just as Martin had said, except it felt as though it was still the middle of the night when a female German guard came into the barracks yelling harshly for everyone to get up. I could hardly move my aching body; my eyes stung from exhaustion.

"We have to get outside for roll call," I heard Martin's sleepy voice urge. "Hurry if you don't want to get a beating." As I struggled to wake up and get myself down from the bunk, I saw Martin take two little boys by the hand and rush for the door. Turning back, he warned me, "Don't ever let a Nazi see that you are wounded, because they might experiment on your leg. They do that a lot with prisoners." He turned and was gone. I nervously followed, trying not to limp or wince from the pain. Any child who fell behind in the rush to line up was kicked or whipped.

We were not allowed to speak with anyone. At all times we had to keep our eyes on the ground. I could see that the guards needed no excuse to beat us. Even a whisper to another prisoner brought a crack with a whip or a blow with a stick. Under the dark skies of early morning, we were a sorrowful bunch, standing in our rows, shivering from the fear and cold. After we were all counted, I could see that there were many, many children in the camp.

A Gestapo officer stepped forward and looked everyone over, telling some of the kids to stand in a row on the side. These were the children that were of no use to the soldiers, who would be sent immediately to the gas chambers. The rest of us were handed a bowl with a little water in it and a chunk of bread that had green mold on it, just like Martin had told us. It made me sick to look at it, but I forced myself to eat it.

Martin was right about the work assignment, too. The kids from our barracks were sent to sort clothes. As we were marched across the open area, Martin said under his breath, "Cato, try to look busy all the time, but work slowly, because if you start out fast, they will give you a lot more to do."

We filed into a large room and saw long tables with conveyor belts in the middle. A guard ordered us to stand on the side of one of the tables and showed us big buckets for men's, women's, and children's clothes. We rummaged through coats, sweaters, skirts, trousers. The Jews had nice clothing. I reached for a small brown skirt. Where was the little girl who had worn this? Could it have belonged to the child whose arms reached for me on the truck? Remembering, I felt dizzy and heartsick.

The first day I didn't dare feel around the hems like Martin had told me to, but I watched as others ducked below the tables and came back up after a few minutes. I could tell that the guards didn't get too close to the ones pretending to throw up. I remembered Martin's words and worked steadily, but not quickly. There was no chance to sit down, get a drink, eat lunch, or go to the outhouse. My mind was exhausted from trying not to think about the people who had worn these clothes. I kept shifting my weight back and forth, trying to find a moment's rest for one aching leg at a time. Many times my legs buckled and I wanted to collapse. Martin read the despair in my face and kept telling me I could make it. Without him, I think I would have given up that first day. I felt like crying, but I remembered my promise that no German would ever see me cry again. By the end of our twelve-hour shift, Rosie looked even paler and weaker.

The guards didn't search anyone leaving the factory that night. As we were marched back to the barracks, Rosie cried constantly and told us she would end up in the gas chamber like her parents. I felt that she was giving up the will to live. I told her she was strong enough to make it and that I needed her, but her eyes gazed off into the distance. My heart was heavy. I, too, was crying, but silently and without tears.

Our supper, if you could call it that, was one ladle of soup as thin as greenish water and a piece of sour, moldy bread. When I looked at the soup that was handed to me, I saw wormlike things floating in the bowl. I asked Martin, "What are they?"

He answered matter-of-factly, "They're maggots."

"Maggots!" I shrieked.

I wanted to throw down the bowl, but Martin grabbed my hand. "Cato," he said sternly, "you better learn to eat what these swine give you or you will be in a grave in no time. You might not believe this, but the more maggots you get in your soup, the more nutrition you get." Fellow prisoners also told me much later that human fat had been used for the soup base. We were starving, so we ate. If anyone ever spilled a drop of soup in the dirt, kids fell to their knees and dug madly for one more drop of nourishment, a maggot, anything.

Our bowls became our most prized possessions. No bowl, no soup. At the entrance of the factory, the guards gave us some water in our bowls, and this would have to last us a whole day. If we spilled it, too bad—they would not give us any more. At night we peed into our bowls and used the warm urine to wash ourselves. The filthy rooms they called bathrooms had one faucet which didn't work most of the time. We were too tired to fight for a drop of water.

The first few days working at the factory were the hardest, until we got used to standing on our feet twelve hours a day with nothing in our bellies. If I could survive one day, perhaps I could survive the next, and the next. It's a good thing I didn't know how many days lay ahead of me in the camp—I might have thrown myself against the electric fence.

During that first week, I was lost in my thoughts when I heard Martin's voice from across the table. "Psst, Cato! Don't forget to check the hems." I glanced at the guard pacing behind Martin, hitting his whip against his hand, scowling as he walked. His eyes were on someone else. I quickly ran my fingers along the bottom of a black skirt like Oma wore, and there it was—a small, hard lump. Nervously, I took a big gulp of air and started to cough and gag. The guard only looked at me with cold disgust. With the skirt up to my mouth, I ducked under the table, making retching sounds and tearing at the hem with my teeth. The slender thread tore easily and I was able to get my fingers around a gold ring with a red stone. I slipped it into my mouth and pulled myself back up to the table, trying to avoid the searching gaze of the guard as he paced back and forth with his whip. I passed the skirt over to the women's bucket. Then I reached for another garment, but was too afraid to search it for hidden treasures. I couldn't control my racing thoughts. This cold ring against my teeth had once adorned someone's finger. Now it would find its way into the hand of a Nazi in exchange for some small favor. Perhaps a grandmother's hands had sewn the ring into the skirt as a last desperate act of love. Had it once been given to her by the hands of someone who loved her?

It took a long time for me to gather the courage to go under the table again with another skirt. I took the ring from my mouth, slipped my hand under my trousers, and shoved the treasure inside my body. That day I escaped a search, also.

Martin was proud of my courage and the treasures I brought back at night. We wrapped the jewelry in an old rag brought back from the clothes sorting, stuffed it in a hole in the corner of the barracks, and covered it with dirt.

Bit by bit over the next several weeks, I picked up information about the camp we had been dumped in. It was called Nordhausen and was located in the Harz Mountains three miles from the town of Nordhausen in eastern Germany. Until October 1944, it was a Buchenwald satellite camp and was also called camp Dora. It then became an independent camp under its own name. Most of the men prisoners were put to work underground in tunnels where V-2 missiles were secretly manufactured. The prisoners who worked in these tunnels had to live in caves dug out of the mountain. Many times dead bodies were brought up from underground. Once in awhile I caught a glimpse of a missile being loaded on a truck. The Nazis had also constructed flimsy barracks, which did little to shut out the cold, and a crematorium.

Roll call came very early every day. We lost track of time, but I think it was about four or five A.M. when we would be ordered to stand outside our barracks in rows of five. Through rain, snow, and wind we stood endlessly. We lost track of time. We learned the trick of puncturing a finger with anything sharp we could find, then smearing the blood on our cheeks to make them look rosy. Within a few days of our arrival, I woke to the horrible discovery that the nameless little girl sleeping next to me had her arms locked around me in death. As I struggled to get free of her icy grip, I called to Martin for help. I tried to shake her to wake her up, but she was stiff all over. We had to drag her body outside with us and hold it up in our row so the count would be correct. After roll call, a guard threw her body onto a nearby stack.

We didn't dare make any friends in the camp, because we never knew if we would see them at the end of the day. With no warning, kids were snatched out of line by guards and we never saw them again. My parents, my friends, and my dear Derk visited me in my dreams, but I always awoke to grim reality. I told Martin about Greet, about Sonja learning to walk, and about the twins I despised. I asked Martin over and over, "Will I ever see Ma and Pa again? Will I ever put skates on my wooden shoes or swim in the canals again?" And the most persistent question, "Will I get to tell the twins what they did to me?"

"Of course you will, Cato," he reassured me. "You are too stubborn to let the Germans kill you. Promise me that no matter what happens, you will never give up without a fight. Someone has to tell the world what happened here."

I promised.

CHAPTER SIXTEEN

I did not weep, and it pained me that I could not weep.
But I had no more tears.

ELIE WIESEL, *NIGHT*

My leg kept festering and dripping with puss until Martin managed to get some water on a rag and cleaned it the best he could. I knew I would have a scar for the rest of my life, how ever long that might be, but that wasn't important enough to care about.

We were allowed to use the outhouses only when we were commanded to. Many of us ended up with diarrhea and couldn't make it to the outhouse. Martin had a solution for this. He helped us find old plastic or rags to tie around our legs. Of course, we smelled terrible and felt as if our skin could crawl away. Our bodies had become so crusted with filth I could not imagine how I could ever get clean again. When the weather turned bitterly cold, I wondered if our layer of filth helped keep us warmer.

We had worked in the factory for about two weeks when Rosie was taken away. She was sent to the other side of the camp where the prisoners had to work in the ovens cleaning up the ashes. As I watched her walking away in a line of children, she glanced back, wearing the saddest look. We knew that she would not be working much longer. Then Piet was sent away to dig ditches for the dead. I think he was chosen because even though his hair that was growing back was very dark from dirt and lice, he still was blonde and clearly not Jewish. Martin told me, "Now you have to bribe some guard with jewelry so they will let you see Piet and Rosie."

Martin and I shared a bunk and talked many times about what we would do when the war was over. We were at the tender age when we should have been going to see movies and dancing and enjoying ourselves. Instead we were struggling to stay alive, growing old before our time.

I learned quickly which guards to "trust" with our bribes. They thought they were the ones watching us, but we were carefully watching them for any sign of humanity. Though we took an awful chance of losing our lives, Martin showed me how to walk by a guard with my hand in my pocket, trying to catch his eye. With a small silent nod, the guard would let me know he was agreeable to a trade. We slipped close by each other, and without looking at his face again, I would draw my hand close to his and soundlessly release my riches to him. Then he would either slip me a crust of bread or a potato, or I would be allowed to leave my area and go in search of Piet or Rosie. The guards must have brought the food with them from their homes. How else would they get it?

We heard that the people who lived in town tried to pretend there was no camp, that there were no people being killed or experimented on. How could they not choke on the clouds of ash and the stench of burning flesh filling the air? What about the guards who went home at night with a ruby or a diamond? What did they tell their wives and children? Did they make up bedtime stories about where they got the jewels, about how many children they had marched into the gas chambers that day and how many limp and lifeless bodies they had carried out?

In spite of how much I loved Rosie, I admit that at first I sometimes felt resentment for the Jews. Just because the Nazis hated them so much, why should we non-Jews have to suffer right along with them? But when the new arrivals came, the little children crying for their parents, I was reminded again that hate knew no borders. The Nazis didn't give a damn who they gassed. Jew or non-Jew, adults or children. If you could hate a child, you could hate anyone.

Every so often a guard pulled me out of my roll-call line to measure my head with a ruler and look me over. He never said a word to me, just measured me and wrote something down. This happened to those of us with blonde hair and blue eyes. I saw a few kids get measured, then taken away, never to come back. If the war had lasted longer, maybe the Nazis would have bred me with someone to have kids that looked Aryan. I was relieved every time to take my place back in line.

We had been prisoners for about three months, every day sorting out the clothing of the new arrivals. I could not imagine where all the people came from. It seemed that every day thousands arrived in those dreadful trains. By now we knew where the weaker ones went. I saw my brother once in a while, always at night. I paid those lousy guards with diamonds so that I could go over to where he was staying, just to exchange a few words. He looked terrible.

Occasionally I would see Rosie from a distance and we raised our hands in greeting. She tried to smile. One night I paid a guard a ruby so I could talk with her for a couple of minutes. She told me, "Cato, it is so hard what I have to do. They are making me work by the ovens, and I see every day how they are burning my people in the ovens. The Germans are so cruel."

"I know," I said. "The other day they set up a show for us all to watch. They must like to brag about what they are doing."

"What happened?" she asked.

I wonder now why I told her what I did. She didn't need to know of more brutality than she witnessed daily. Perhaps it was so that she would know I shared in her abhorrence of the cruelty being carried out on her people. I told her about three men who were punished because they had drawn an escape plan. The men were hung upside down on a crossbar with their legs tied back against their thighs and their hands tied behind their backs. A female Nazi stuck a sharpened wooden stick through their rectums and the stick came out through their testicles. She just left them there to die while we watched helplessly. "Rosie," I seethed, "the men's screams were so terrible. Those bastards! I wish I was strong enough to kill them all myself."

Rosie's pale face became twisted with anger. "Someday they will be punished for what they are doing."

"Yeah, sure," I said bitterly. "But what about in the meantime? If there is a God, why doesn't he stop them now?"

No one could ever answer that question. As the guard I had bribed signaled it was time for me to leave, Rosie touched my hand and said a soft good-bye. Walking through the mud to my barracks, I felt my heart weep. No matter how tough I thought my shell was, Rosie got through. How could a heart as hardened and scarred as mine begin to break again whenever I saw her?

Besides bribing the guards, Martin taught us another way to scrounge extra food for our hollow bellies. He told us to follow what he called "muzzlemen," prisoners who had given up and just walked aimlessly about the camp waiting to die. Sometimes they still had a piece of bread from roll call in their pockets and instead of eating, they would just lie down and die. One afternoon I saw a man stumbling around on two legs that were nothing but bones. I couldn't tell how old he was. He disappeared behind one of the barracks. I thought he must be one of those muzzlemen Martin had told us about. I checked quickly to see if any of the guards were watching me, but could see no one. I sneaked around the building where the man had fallen down. When I came up to him, he was lying on the dirt, his sunken eyes open and staring. I knew they were the eyes of death. I sat down next to him and big tears ran down my face. I know I had said no German would ever see me cry again but this man was not a German.

I leaned over and closed his eyes and cried to him, "Yes, Mister, I am glad it is over for you. You are out of this place." I crouched there talking to a dead person, until I suddenly thought, Cato, have you gone so crazy that you talk to a dead man? Get yourself together. This man is never going to answer you. Look for some food. Take his clothing, it is no good to him anymore. I dug around in his pockets and was lucky— he had a piece of black bread on him. I wolfed it down, vowing that the next piece I found would be saved for Piet and Martin. Then I removed his clothing. I could feel the clammy body underneath my small hands, hoping in a way he would not give up so easily, that he would kick and fight for his life. But no, he had to die on me.

By this time I had seen so many people naked that it didn't bother me to see this one. I stuffed his clothing under mine and walked away without glancing back. The extra clothing would keep me a little warmer. The double layer also made us look well-fed when underneath, our skin hung on our ribs. Anything to look healthy enough not to be killed.

After so many months, Piet was starting to give up. He told me he couldn't take it any longer. His job was digging ditches and throwing the bodies in, sometimes hundreds at a time. I shook him hard and said, "Don't you dare give up on me. This war is going to be over someday and you and I are going to tell the world about these camps." He wouldn't look me in the eye.

"Martin is helping me a lot, you know," I went on. "Do you want me to see if he can come over to see you?"

"Yeah, sure, you do what you want," he mumbled, staring at the ground.

I grabbed his arm and shook it hard, forcing him to look at me. "You know, Piet, no one has it any easier. I stand on my feet for twelve hours a day sorting out clothes that once belonged to someone who was alive, who had kids. I smell the death all around me, too, just like you," I said angrily. Piet's sharp tongue had snapped me out of passivity in the past. I had to snap him out of this spell of resignation that had come over him. I never used to care if I made him mad before; I wasn't going to start now.

"I know, Cato," he said in agony, as if his words burned his mouth so bitterly that he could hardly say them. "But you don't have to touch the dead bodies like I do. You don't have to look at their faces." He glanced bitterly at the Nazi across the square. "Do you know that before they put them in the ovens they have people opening up the mouths and

141

pulling out gold teeth with pliers so the Germans can have all that gold made into something for their families!" His voice cracked. I knew that just as I had, Piet had learned to cry in silence, without tears.

Rosie worked in the area of the ovens through autumn and long into the biting winter. I had seen her every few weeks for a few clandestine moments. Then one day as we left work I saw her trudging along in what I called the "death line." Until the day I die the look she had in her eyes will haunt me. It told me that she was glad that it was over and that at last she could go the same way her parents had gone. Anything, her face said, would be better than this camp of horrors she lived in now.

I felt no pride that I lived while those around me were dying. I could take no pride in the Aryan features that protected me while the dark-complected Jewish children were destroyed by the hundreds. But there was more—Rosie's heart was softer than mine. It finally broke, while mine grew harder and more stubborn. I don't think she knew how to hate. I watched as the more tenderhearted, delicate children died around me. I watched others grow more calloused and unfeeling. I feared the kind of world we would inhabit when all the Rosies were gone and only those of us who were tough enough had survived. Was my gentle friend one of the lucky ones after all?

After seeing Rosie for the last time I stumbled back to my barracks in a heavy cloud of grief. Night began to close in around me. I had just cut behind one of the buildings when a German soldier suddenly confronted me. "What are you doing here?" he barked. I froze in my tracks. Knowing I would be punished severely for being there and still stunned by Rosie's imminent death, I mustered all my hate for everything he stood for and blurted out, *"Du bist verruckt, das Schwein!"* (You are damned, you pig!) As I turned to walk away, the man grabbed me, pulled me around and threw me on the ground. His face was fiery red, his breath hot against my face. I felt his coarse hands pulling at my clothes. *"Bitte, bitte, nein!"* (Please, please, no!) I pleaded, trying to push him away with arms like twigs against his monstrous strength. His heavy body trapped me against the ground and the realization of what he was doing to me pierced me like a dagger. I pinched my eyes closed to try to black out what was happening. When the filthy soldier was through with me, I watched him walk away with a grin on his face. He had done something so terrible to my body I wanted to peel away every piece of skin his hands had touched. I swore I would kill him. But I didn't let him see me cry.

It took all my strength to get to my feet. I staggered toward my barracks, bruised, broken, and dirty. The beast had smeared me with a kind of dirt I could never wash away. As soon as Martin saw me, he seemed to know what had happened. Silently he pulled me close to him and held me for the longest time. I tried to find a way to tell him what had happened, but he gently put his finger on my mouth to stop me. "I think I know. You don't have to tell me," he said. My thoughts were spinning with images of the soldier, his hideous body, of Pa's hands inside my bathing suit, of rats and slime.

"Oh, Martin," I gasped, "what if I have a baby from that swine?"

"I don't think it's possible because you are too undernourished," Martin said. "Those swine have raped many of the girls, but I don't think they have had babies."

Martin still held me. "It was bound to happen eventually. Be careful. Don't trust any of the guards, even the ones who take our bribes. Don't ever get caught behind a building with one of them. If one tries to get close to you, get out of his way. And Cato, be grateful you're not a Jew."

"What does it matter if I'm a Jew or not? I'm suffering just the same."

He retorted, "Yes, but at least we're not ending up in the ovens like they do."

"Well, maybe we should, Martin. Then at least it would be over. We have to live to see these damn animals torture people. At least when these people die, it is over for them. Me, I am never going to forget the things that have happened. I wish sometimes they would put us in the ovens."

Martin's voice was angry. "Don't you ever talk that way again, Cato. You're going to get out of here. Remember what you have told me and what you tell Piet?"

"Yes, I remember," I sighed. "But it's so hard to live with death around you day after day."

That night I cried myself to sleep, unable to forget Rosie's vacant eyes or my degradation. Little did I realize I would be abused by many more guards before I was free.

CHAPTER SEVENTEEN

Humor is a prelude to faith and
Laughter is the beginning of prayer.

REINHOLD NIEBUHR

Our rare moments of triumph and laughter shine in my memory like a distant flickering star in a black sky. I wanted to be able to make Martin feel some hope amid all the sorrow. "Hey, do you know what I found the other day?" I asked him one night. "I was sorting out some clothes when I felt a hard piece. I ducked below the table, but I had trouble ripping the hem open with my teeth because they hurt so much. Do you think I'm going to lose my teeth, Martin?"

"I'm going to be a doctor, not a dentist, Cato. Get on with your story."

"Well, this guard must have thought I was down there a long time, so he came over to where I was. He yells *'Was ist los?'* (What is wrong?) and I just pretended I couldn't hear him. Boy, you should have seen me. I really put out the puking sounds. I guess it was so sickening for the poor man's stomach he walked away. I finally managed to get the hem ripped open and found this nice ruby in it."

"What did you do with it?"

"I stuck it up inside me and brought it back and buried it. It will come in handy sometime. You know in the beginning I thought it was sickening to do this, but I don't care any more. Maybe we're turning into animals, do you think?" I asked him.

"No, we aren't," he insisted. "After this war is over, we are going to get back to being human beings again and live normal lives. The only animals around here are Nazis, and I sure wouldn't have one of them for a pet," laughed Martin.

"I wouldn't either," I agreed. "But I can tell you if I did I would bring him to a doctor and tell him to put this animal to sleep. And make sure he suffers a lot." Both of us had a good laugh. Seeing Martin smile was my only delight.

"You know, this ruby should be worth something to one of those louses. I'm going to save it as long as I can. Then maybe I can get one to bring me a potato for it." The guards were like crows—they loved anything shiny. "You know, I wonder how their families feel when they get home from work," I said.

"What do you mean?"

"I wonder if their wife or kids ask, 'Did you have a nice day, love? What did you do today, Papa?'" I said with a mocking voice. " 'I killed one hundred Jews today, my darling.'"

"You're crazy, Cato!" Martin said.

"I know it, but this place makes me crazy," I sighed. It was a relief to have a laugh now and then; it gave us a bit of strength for the days ahead. For a moment, I could feel like the little girl I still was.

It helped, too, to tell Martin about Greet and Sonja. Not long before I was taken to Nordhausen, Greet and I put a "peek-a-boo" box to good use. A peek-a-boo box was a shoe box with a little window cut in one end with a curtain over it. Inside we had drawn scenery of trees and mountains and glued down little wooden figures. Mine were the only pretty things I had ever made. Greet and I had learned to make them at school, and since we weren't afraid of strangers, we decided to make peek-a-boo boxes and ask people on the street to pay us for a peek. If we asked enough people, somebody always found a one-cent piece in a pocket to pay us for a peek and gave us a pat on the head. We glued a little matchbox on the side to keep our money in. The rattle of the coins in the matchbox made me feel rich enough to shout.

After the war started, we got sick of seeing German soldiers strut around our streets without our being able to tell them where to go. As we walked by the canal one morning, we thought of our best trick ever.

We rushed home to get a potato sack, ran back and dipped it in the water. Before long, the current carried a perfect sized rat right into the sack. We cinched the top of the sack and squeezed the water out of the burlap. Greet held on to the wiggling bag and I held a newly constructed peek-a-boo box with one hand and its lid in the other. This one had no scenery or figures or even a matchbox or decorations on the outside because we knew we could only use it once. As Greet dumped the clawing, squirming rat into the open box, I clamped the lid on like lightning and held it tight. We tied string around it, then went in search of a customer, the rat scraping the sides to find an escape.

Greet saw the Nazi first. He stood waiting for a streetcar on the next corner. We turned on our charm and smiled sweetly.

"Sir, would you like to take a peek in our box for a cent?" I asked in a sugary voice in the best German I could muster.

"There's a pretty surprise behind the curtain," Greet chimed in, tilting her head just so.

He seemed to understand what we were after and dug into his pocket for a coin. I could feel laughter welling up inside, but I didn't let my face show it. He handed me his money. I handed him the box.

As he lifted it for his peek, Greet and I made a run for it, not daring to look back. Safely around the closest building, we grabbed each other and almost fell over with laughter. Greet tried to keep me from peeking around the bricks, but I couldn't resist. No soldier in sight. No rat. The box lay in the street, to be crushed under the traffic. We were so mad we didn't get to see the look on his face when he peeked in.

At Nordhausen, we saved up our lice in a small matchbox that some German had tossed on the ground. We filled this box with hundreds of them. After all, we had plenty more where they came from. The lice dug themselves deep into the open sores that covered our bodies. While someone distracted him, I'd creep up behind a soldier and empty our matchbox on his clothes. We joked that they should be sharing some of our "pets." It was such a small way to get back at the guards, but it made us feel like we had enough spirit left to fight back. Greet would have been proud, I'm sure.

I shared this story with Piet when I saw him. After I finished talking, Piet asked me, "Do you still see Martin?"

"Yes," I told him. "He's still in the same barracks I am and we are good friends. He helps everyone, no matter how bad he feels."

Piet told me sadly that he didn't have any friends on his side of the camp. He had decided it was bad luck for anyone to be his friend because he had seen so many people he talked to be beaten to death. What was the use of making any if they would all end up in a hole anyway.

It wasn't only my stubbornness or my hate for the Germans or my dreams of revenge that kept me alive. It was also my love for Martin. Through all the misery we tried to see our future ahead. We knew we would work together to cure and help people someday. A friend like Martin was more precious than any diamond or ruby. He was more precious than life itself, for he gave me life in a world of death.

Interruptions from our work became routine. One day we were pulled out to see a young woman accused of being a spy. She stood trembling between two Gestapo agents. She was a Jew we knew had been raped by several of the guards. In her arms she clutched her newborn baby boy. Another soldier pulled the screaming infant from her and held the baby upside down by its feet and began swinging him back and forth. The little boy cried weakly as his mother wept and reached out to protect her son. But they didn't care. One of the men took his knife and sliced off the baby's ear. Blood dripped from the tiny head onto the soldier's boot, which seemed to annoy him. So he swung the baby again and sliced off the other ear. If one of us dropped our heads to shut out the horror, a guard barked at us to keep our eyes on the boy.

The mother lay in the dirt. Tears poured down my cheeks, my pledge forgotten. I could hear sobbing all around me. The soldier proceeded to slice this tiny child to pieces, hacking away until it finally died.

Then we were allowed to go back to work. I could taste the hate I felt, but there wasn't anything I could do about it. We never saw the mother again. Knowing the Nazis like I did, I was sure she died that day, too. The baby's bloodstains in the dirt seemed to last forever. I walked by them morning and night, unable to forget. Even after they were gone.

We had been in the camp for about fourteen months when Martin, Piet, and I were talking about how more and more packed trains were arriving and more and more killings seemed to be happening faster and faster.

"What's going on?" I asked Piet. "Have you heard or seen anything?"

"I've heard some talk from other prisoners that Hitler is losing the war."

"What do you mean?" I pressed him. What was I hearing? Could this be possible?

"I heard that he has been pushed out of Italy and has lost France already. I don't know anything about Holland."

My whole body was tingling. "But Piet, Holland is right next to France. Maybe it's free, too! Martin, have you heard anything about this?" I asked, feeling my first real hope in months.

"Oh, I heard about it," he answered glumly.

I grabbed his shoulders and shook him. "Why didn't you tell me about it then? I think that's mean!"

"Cato, I didn't want to get your hopes up. Hitler is killing more Jews than ever," he added darkly. "Look around. He still has plenty of people doing what he tells them. He is not going to lose this war."

"Maybe Hitler thinks that he might lose the war and he better not leave any witnesses around," Piet said.

"But Piet," I said as fear quickly buried my hope, "that means they'll kill us too because we know what they are doing!"

"We just have to hope they don't, Cato," Piet said, but there was not a trace of hope in his voice.

"This will all be for nothing if they kill us now. Someone has to stay alive to tell the world what has happened," I said, growing more and more upset.

"I don't know, Cato, I just don't know," Piet muttered and turned to leave, as the guard signaled for us to end our visit.

Martin and I walked back through the black sludge past corpses stacked ten feet high against the fences. Feces oozed from the bodies, maggots crawled in and out of their eyes and noses and mouths. The rank odor was so nauseating that someone who has never breathed it cannot imagine it. I had seen so much death, that I could walk by with no feeling. "Martin," I said, "from now on, when you hear anything, anything at all, I want you to tell me. Now tell me, what have you heard?"

"I overheard a new prisoner talking about France and Italy."

"Did you ask about Holland, Martin? What about Holland?" I asked anxiously.

"I couldn't ask. They didn't know I was listening or whether I was a spy."

I felt so old and worn out lying beside the other kids in my bunk that night. My brain was working feverishly. I have to get out of here, I thought. I have to get back to Holland. Were Greet and Sonja still alive? What about my folks? Were they ever told where I was taken? And what about my cat, Mollie? I wanted to be a teenager, to live free without any Krauts around, without the stench of death in every breath. I had to get away from the screaming.

My thoughts turned to Henny and Jenny. I didn't want them hung until I got back to Amsterdam. I wanted to be their hangman.

I became obsessed with survival.

CHAPTER EIGHTEEN

*I went to Auschwitz . . . and was shown the many exhibits
. . . that leave nothing to be added concerning the evil
human beings can do to other human beings. But the one
that left the most profound impression on me was the sim-
plest of all: a room full of shoes, mostly baby shoes.*

ROBERT JAY LIFTON

One bitter winter day, we were ordered away from our clothes sorting, out into the biting wind to "watch" something. Another lesson, I groaned. To make us stronger, the guards said. What was it this time? In the middle of the square stood a transport truck filled with babies. A guard stood on the truck, tossing the tiny naked bodies into a pile on the ground as if they were stones.

"Martin," I asked desperately, "whose babies are these?"

"They're Jewish and Gypsy babies."

"But the babies haven't done anything wrong."

"I know it, and you know it. But they're the children of Jews and Gypsies and the Nazis want to get rid of them."

At least it's over for them, I thought. They don't have to live in this stinking world. But something I saw sent shock waves through me. Some of the babies were still moving, still alive! And in between the obscene shouting of the guards, an occasional whimper broke through. I froze. These babies were still alive, so very cold, and in the hands of the Nazis!

"What are they going to do with them?" I asked Martin.

"Some they use for experiments. I saw them pour bleach into a baby's eyes once to try to change the color."

This Martin had not warned me about. I watched the soldiers light a fire. Once the fire was blazing high enough, they ordered us to throw the babies into the flames. I couldn't move. I just stared at the emaciated little bodies. With his whip poised in the air ready to strike, a soldier marched toward us. Martin bent over to pick up a lifeless infant and threw it into the fire, where the flames instantly engulfed it. The German stepped toward me, screaming. I saw the threat of my own death in his face. I picked up a body, not like the soldiers picked the babies up by the foot or hand, but with my two trembling hands so I could cradle its head. It was so very light in my arms, as if I held a shadow. The baby boy's eyes were closed, and I was quite sure he was dead. The soldier raised his whip again. In utter agony, I released my hold on the infant and threw him into the inferno. The hellish light and scorching heat seared forever into my memory the sight of the flames devouring him.

The soldiers' laughter engulfed me in fury. I wanted to heave the men into the fire. I wanted to see them shrink in the flames and hear their skin sizzle and watch their faces twist as they were consumed. I reached for another baby and threw it. Martin threw several more as the smoke and stink of the fire grew. The guards laughed at our torment, insulting us, cursing us, saying these Jewish babies were no more than animals, that we should be ashamed of our weakness. Bending down to pick up another infant, I heard a cry.

I looked into the child's face and saw that it was still alive. Grief, pain, and fear overwhelmed me as I stared into its eyes. I did not want to believe that it was still alive, or accept what this meant. The guards yelled at me to hurry, and Martin looked over and saw that the baby was moving.

"Cato, you know what to do," Martin said.

Martin was wrong. I did not know what to do. I turned and looked at him, holding the baby's body against mine. The guards yelled at me again.

I heard the cry again, a soft, pitiful, kittenlike cry. The infant's eyes were too large in its emaciated face, its body frail and stiff with fear. "Twist the neck," Martin said, "or it will suffer."

I stared at him. The guards lunged toward me. Martin's mouth shaped his urgent message, "Hurry!"

I looked down and saw the little mouth open and heard a thousand voices, a million voices, moaning. The little head turned to one side, quickly, yet seeming to take minutes, and I saw my hand go down to its throat. Another faint cry escaped and filled my head with a deafening roar. My hand on its throat tightened.

I could do this. I could squeeze the life and pain out of this frail body, or I could throw it alive into the fire. Or I could refuse and be beaten, tortured, then thrown into the fire myself. A tide of agony welled within me. The roar echoed in my mind, shaking my body. I turned my head from the child, unable to look into its eyes again, and felt the hand squeeze the throat as hard as it could. I twisted its neck and mechanically threw the limp body end over end into the fire.

Behind my tough and calloused shell, my heart crumbled.

The guard seemed satisfied and turned his attention to someone else. Through the flames I saw the little baby's arms and legs twisting in the heat. And I heard its cries.

No! The baby could not be screaming! I squeezed the life out of it. I broke its neck. Still I heard the deafening screams of a little baby, of many babies, and I looked around, stunned. Other children had been called out of the barracks and stood now near the fire, surrounded by the babies they were throwing into the pit. Live babies, dead babies. The cries were from the infants in the fire. Horrified, I watched the suffering children writhe in the flames.

"Arbeit!" (Work!) screamed a guard, not five feet behind me. I grabbed another body and threw it into the blistering fire. I reached for another baby, this one also dead, and tossed it onto the heap. The screams, the cries were everywhere, rising toward heaven with the ashes of innocence. Tiny arms and legs flailed against the agony until they were stilled by death.

How could the Nazis stand it? How could they laugh? I saw Martin twist a little child's neck and throw it into the fire. Another baby moved in my arms. I saw its eyes plead with me to help it, to love it, to save it. I turned my head away so I couldn't see as I twisted its delicate neck. My arms numbly threw it to its fiery grave. I felt something die in me.

Every baby was destroyed.

A different girl walked back to the workroom to sort clothes. A different girl stood at the table and held in her hand a tiny white dress, worn perhaps that morning by one of the babies. The child sorting clothes was only thirteen years old, but she had borne the anguish of the ages. She had taken life. She had become a murderer.

I would never, ever, be the same.

I did not speak another word that day until I got back to the barracks with Martin.

As the other children climbed into their bunks, Martin said, "Let's you and I sit over by that wall and talk for awhile." He put his arm around my waist, I put my head on his shoulder. We sat down in the dirt and I cried. My heart let go and my body obligingly produced the tears I hoped could carry away the hot grief. But so much of it burned inside that it just kept coming and coming and coming until there were no tears left. My heart took over and kept emptying itself. At least the suffering of the babies was over. They were free, with my friend Rosie. I was so glad for a friend like Martin who gave me strength even when I know he felt as terrible as I did.

It was deathly quiet in the barracks that night. I knew everyone was thinking about the same thing.

My determination to endure only increased after seeing those babies murdered. I went over and over in my mind what I had seen and how I wanted to see the twins suffer when we were set free. Henny and Jenny became the maggots I had to eat in my soup. They were the cold slime that was slick on my bread in the mornings. I had never felt such hate coursing through my body.

The next time I bribed my way to see Piet I gave him a crust of bread I had taken off a corpse. "It won't do any good," he told me. "This puny piece of bread won't help because eventually we are all going to be dead."

"Piet!" I yelled, grabbing his arm and jerking it hard. "You listen to me. We are not going to die, you understand me? Don't you dare give up, because if you do, then so will I. We've been here a long time and we are still alive! We all look like death and my stomach has shrunk so much I don't even miss food anymore, but we're alive."

"Cato," he said in a flat, lifeless voice, "you have no idea what it's like to do what I have to do." He sounded like an old man.

"Oh, shut up, Piet! Just because I work in a factory doesn't mean I don't know what is going on over here on the other side of the camp."

"Do you know what I had to do yesterday?" he asked, his voice rising in despair. "I had to stand on top of the warm bodies that had been tossed into a hole I dug. Some of the kids were still alive because their parents had protected them from the Germans' bullets with their bodies," he sobbed, letting me see him cry for the first time in his life. I didn't dare tell him what I had seen and been forced to do. I couldn't let him know how close I had come to giving up. He took the piece of bread and slipped it in his pocket without looking at it. He was no longer the Piet I had known—part of him had died, too.

Day after grinding day we stood at the work tables, watchful and weary. I became quite proficient at detecting gems and fooling the guards with my "sickness." Our stash of jewelry kept us supplied with bribes. The only breaks in the deadly routine were the punishments the guards poured down on us or the times they took us outside to watch one of their sadistic exhibitions. Always, these were supposed to teach us a lesson. What the lesson was I didn't know. They had to have an audience. The only lesson I learned was how unspeakably evil the Nazis could be. And I thought they were very stupid to insist on witnesses to every atrocity, because maybe someday, somehow, someone would escape and tell the world what they had done.

For no reason I could figure out, the guards would suddenly grab one of us while we were working and march us over to the wall. It seemed to take hardly anything to make a Nazi mad, and if one was in a bad mood, then watch out. No matter how hard I tried to keep from being noticed, many times I was one of those ordered to stand with my hands behind my back, my nose one inch from the wall. If we swayed at all or let our noses touch the wall, the whips snapped against our shoulders. For three hours or more at a time, we would have to stand perfectly still. If we moved the least bit, the guards took delight in pulling us away from the wall and beating us mercilessly.

Once, to "teach us a lesson," we were marched outside to see two girls, not much older than I, tied to some kind of hospital table. I saw in their faces the bone-chilling fear we had known and seen every day in the camp—cold, paralyzing, choking terror, born of what we had witnessed. The girls' eyes grew wider with horror as two doctors, or perhaps just men in white coats, approached them, knives in hand. Each "doctor" took a girl, roughly held down her exposed leg, and with no anesthetic of any kind, sliced a bloody gash down her thigh. Blood gushed from the huge incisions. I gripped Martin's arm to keep from sinking to the ground in despair. There was no escape. Thrashing, screaming, the girls struggled to get away, but even if they could have escaped their bonds, there was nowhere to go. Filthy rags that had been soaked in a bucket of machine oil were stuffed into the raw wounds, then the butchers stitched them up, leaving the legs unbandaged. The girls were untied and their torturers simply walked away and left them alone in their agony. Somewhere I heard this justified as a medical experiment to learn about wounds that German soldiers might suffer on the battlefield.

In an icy metallic voice, a guard announced that the same thing would be done to us if we tried to escape or did anything to anger a guard. Trudging back to the factory after the ordeal, Martin shuddered. "Those girls are not going to live long. Their legs will get gangrene in them and they will be sent to the gas chamber."

That night I feared that even Martin was giving up. As we lay in our bunk, I cried about the girls we had seen. "Oh, Martin," I wept. "Don't the Nazis have any feelings?"

He said nothing. My fears overflowed into a torrent of words mixing with my tears. "Martin, are we ever going to get out of here? Will I ever see Mollie again or Ma and Pa? And what about Derk and my friends? You want to be a doctor and you know so much, but do you think that we'll be so sick we'll never grow up even if we get out?"

Slowly and with great weariness, Martin answered me. "I have no idea, Cato. There is so much to learn and I am so tired. Maybe you're right. Maybe we won't ever get out of here alive."

Panic seized me like a hand clutching my throat. "Martin," I screamed, pummeling his chest with my fists, "don't you dare say that. I hate you for saying that. We are going to get out of here, you hear!" I cried, I pleaded. "Please, Martin, don't say that ever again," I begged. "You know we have a life outside. You and I are going to be together. I'm going to be your nurse, remember?"

"I hope you're right, Cato. I know I should be braver, but it is so hard. Some days are worse than others." Now it was my turn to be strong for Martin. I stopped crying and held him until he fell asleep.

CHAPTER NINETEEN

*Have we ever thought about the consequence of a horror
that . . . is yet the worst of all to those of us who have
faith: the death of God in the soul of a child who
suddenly discovers absolute evil?*

FRANCOIS MAURIAC

As time went on we could tell that something was bothering the soldiers. They seemed even more short-tempered than usual. More and more Jews arrived at the camp; more and more were sent to the showers. The ovens were operating around the clock now. It was hard to breathe with so much death in the air.

I had no idea there were so many Jews.

It seemed like every day we were forced to witness more Nazi cruelty. I was becoming so hardened to all the blood and death that it seemed to bother me less as the days passed. Whenever Martin or someone else would talk about being set free, I got furious because it was obviously not going to happen. And I had seen enough that I would never try to escape.

One afternoon we had heard a big commotion outside the factory. As soon as we were herded outside, I knew we were going to be taught another lesson. The Nazis had caught a few men and a woman who had supposedly tried to escape. The prisoners sat in chairs with their hands tied to some kind of torture machine. Their fingers were spread apart, with a screw tightened over each finger so they couldn't pull their hands out. A guard took a huge hammer and slammed it down onto the contraption so that each finger was broken. When the guards tightened the thumbscrews, blood spurted from the victims' fingers. Their fingers were nothing but bloody pulp after the Nazis got through with them. The guards looked on with amusement, then shouted for us to return to work.

At roll call on another gray, wet morning, a guard yelled at several rows of five to follow him. What did we have to watch now? Would it never end? But he led us across the field toward the ovens, which were actually in camp Dora. I held on to Martin, "Oh God, Martin, it's our turn! They're going to burn us now," I moaned. We stood there filthy, arms and legs like sticks, bellies bloated like melons. I had the crazy thought that if the Gestapo's dogs had tried to kill us, they wouldn't even get a nice juicy bone to chew on. As we approached the ovens, I was shaking so hard I thought I would die of fright before they killed me. Our fight was over. Tears coursed through the dirt on our cheeks. Holding on to Martin, I cried, "Good-bye. Maybe I'll see you in another world." I remember Martin rubbing his eyes so hard the dirt was smeared across his face. He looked at me in mute despair.

Oh, help me, Martin, I thought. You are the only one who can save us, but how I do not know. I thought of the God my Oma had told me about. How could I pray for deliverance from a God who had watched Rosie die? Who had let babies burn? Who had not struck Hitler dead with His mighty hand? I had heard the prayers of hundreds of Jews as they went to their deaths. I had nothing to say to Him. Knowing this was my final moment of life, I kept my eyes on Martin's beloved face, so that my last memory would be of him. A soldier stepped toward us brandishing his whip. Take us together, I thought. Don't let me die without Martin.

The soldier barked at us to start cleaning out the ovens. It was just a new job! We were still good for something so they weren't going to kill us, not yet. Maybe they would kill us after our work, but I didn't care anymore. I felt dizzy and weak.

I had never dared to get close to the long row of ovens before. I had only seen their red bricks and huge smokestack from a distance. It had scared me to know that so many people were burned here. The ovens were clogged with the bones and ashes from an endless stream of bodies. In each oven, the ashes must have been two or three feet high. The heat from the brick walls suddenly reminded me of the bakery wall that had warmed a life that now seemed long ago. Were the ashes of my friends Hans and Jopie in an oven somewhere?

Our assignment was to shovel the ashes into wheelbarrows, all the while choking on the smoke and dust. Older prisoners emptied the ashes into trucks which took them somewhere to be dumped. I knew I stood knee-deep in powdery ash that had once been human beings. I was only making room for the next load of bodies. It left me cold; I had no tears left.

That night, Piet managed to get through to our barracks. I was so glad to see him, I threw my arms around his neck. But Piet was deeply depressed. He was fading. Desperately he said, "They made me do something terrible today, Cato."

"Me too," I said. "I had to clean out the ovens."

Not hearing me, he went on in a hollow voice. "Something's up. Have you heard anything more, Martin? Do you know what happened where I work? I had to dig even deeper trenches this time. The Gestapo brought a bunch of Jews to the edge and made them kneel down with their hands tied behind their backs. Then they shot them all in the back of the neck."

"We've seen that, too, Piet," Martin said.

"But when those men fell in, they brought another row of Jews and shot them. They kept shooting and shooting until there must have been five hundred men in those ditches."

I gagged.

Piet continued with the voice of an old man, "But that isn't all. In another pit they threw in live Jews on top of the dead ones. Then they poured petrol over them and set fire to them. You should have heard all the screaming coming out of that hole, those bastards. They kept saying it was done by orders of the Führer."

It was no wonder Piet looked like he did.

I could feel spring coming, but it didn't matter. Train after train rumbled into camp. Many of them packed with prisoners from other camps. After days without food or water, few were still alive. The walking dead were forced to toss out the bodies of their friends who had perished in the boxcars. The merciless routine continued. Up at four or five in the morning. Guards shouting. Roll call in the rain, standing sometimes two or three hours waiting for what, I don't know. Every minute trying to think of home, my friends, Mollie, anything but what was happening to me. Soggy, moldy bread, maggot soup. Kids kept dying and we propped them up in line until a guard dragged them away. Ashes filled what little hair we had with a fine gray powder. Our faces were black with soot. We could hear airplanes and bombs, but we paid no attention to them any longer. What was the use? Getting killed by a stray bomb would be better than this. For some reason, the guards had quit taking bribes from our storehouse of jewelry, so I could not see Piet. The guards seemed to be less cruel, somehow distracted by an urgency to speed up the killings. As we loaded the countless corpses into the ovens, human flesh fell off in our hands. The ten ovens burned around the clock, feeding their smoke into one immense smoke stack that blackened the sky with a noxious cloud.

Lost in my gruesome task one morning, I was startled by the sound of shouting. Not the harsh shouting of the guards telling us to hurry, but of young voices, and in their midst, Martin's voice was calling my name. He rushed up to me, breathless.

"It's over! It's over! Cato, the war is over! Germany has lost the war!" he yelled, picking me up and swinging me around. I had never seen such a smile on his face.

As he let me down, I tried to get my balance. "Are you sure, Martin?" I asked wearily. I'd heard all this before.

"Yes, I'm sure. Come on over to the gate," he urged, pulling my hands.

Stubbornly, I held my ground. "I don't believe it. It's just another lie. And we better get back to work or we'll get beaten up, and you know it." I glanced fearfully around to see which guards might be threatening. But I couldn't see any guards, or any dogs. Where were they? Could Martin be right? No, it couldn't be. It was all a dream and soon I would wake up to find myself facing a whip.

"Hit me or pinch me so I'll know I'm awake," I said.

"You're awake, Cato. The Americans are a few miles from here and they're coming to set us free. We're going home!" he squealed. I still could not believe the unbelievable, but how desperately I wanted to. Martin tugged on my arm, and I followed, half-willingly at first, then faster as I sensed the excitement of the others.

Running arm in arm, dodging frantic prisoners, and watching for guards, we tried to find Piet. I don't know how our feeble bodies had the energy, but run we did. The few Nazi soldiers I did see were not watching us. They were looking scared, running around like headless chickens.

"Hey, stop, Martin! Stop for a minute." I dug my heels into the dirt and pulled him back.

"Why? Are you crazy or something?"

"I want to kill one of those bastards right now, before the Americans get here. Will you help me?" It was a crazy idea, but my pounding heart told me I had the strength to tear one of those hated guards to pieces.

"No, let the Americans take care of them. We've got to get out of here."

We found Piet still digging a trench, unaware of the news. He didn't realize that his guards, too, had deserted their posts. I let go of Martin and ran ahead to Piet, screaming hysterically, "Piet, Piet, the war is over! We're free! The Americans are coming!" I tried to grab his shovel away from him and throw it down.

"Cato, stop it," he growled. "Don't believe that stupid rumor. Get out of here or you'll get shot, too."

"Piet," I exploded, clutching his arm. "All the guards are running away. The Germans have lost the war." His arm was no bigger around than the shovel handle.

Piet's eyes widened as he looked around in disbelief. Not a single guard in sight. Other children who also trusted Martin had followed us and were clamoring in hopeful confusion. "Be quiet, everyone," Martin shouted, holding his hand in the air. "Listen! Can't you hear that sound?

It's heavy trucks and they're getting closer! It must be the Americans." I had heard those sounds in Amsterdam when the Nazis thundered through the streets rounding up Jews as if they were stray dogs. I'd heard them the night of the party, above the cries of hundreds of children. It was a sound I feared and despised.

I had not seen a smile on Piet's terribly thin face for months, but a grin fought against his doubt and finally won. He threw down his shovel and took my hand. "C'mon Cato! Let's go see!"

The crowd of children ran toward the barbed wire fence, instinctively stopping just short of its deadly metal strands. We saw our guards on the other side, running who knows where as fast as they could. It was a wonderful sight. I wanted to see bullet holes in their backs.

We heard the rumble of trucks getting closer and closer. Everything was chaos and confusion. As we made our way to the gate, I felt my feet slow down with apprehension. I had no idea what an American looked like. How could we be sure the trucks weren't loaded with German reinforcements? I watched as a huge, green truck stopped right outside the open gates and soldiers jumped out of the cab. As they looked around, they called to each other in a language I had never heard. What were they saying to each other? Their uniforms and helmets were very different from what the Germans wore.

Maybe Martin had been wrong and these soldiers were here to take us to another camp to finally be tortured to death. I reached for Martin's protecting arms, but he wasn't there. I whirled around, searching the crowd of ragged prisoners, but I couldn't see him anywhere.

"Martin!" I screamed frantically. "Where are you?" All around me were prisoners, some holding on to each other for support, some crying, some making a sound I had not heard from them—laughter. Some just stared blankly at me from skeletal faces, as if they did not comprehend what was happening. No one answered. Where could Martin be? Don't tell me that after all this, the Germans got hold of him! "Martin!" I yelled again. But no answer, no sign of the face that had been my beacon of

When Nordhausen was liberated, the living lay amongst the dead.

A U.S. soldier watches citizens of Nordhausen ordered to dig graves for a mass burial of 2500 dead prisoners from the concentration camp located outside their town.

UPI/Bettmann Newsphotos. Used with permission.

hope through twenty months of hell. My eyes searched among the hundreds of soldiers that had emerged from the trucks and tanks. Perhaps Martin had already gotten out.

Some of the Americans knelt in the dirt, stretching their arms toward the timid children. A few already held children on their knees. I walked slowly forward, edging my way closer and closer to the soldiers, pulling Piet with me, not trusting anyone. What I saw next surprised me. Several of the soldiers were crying. One of them knelt in front of Piet and me and pulled from his jacket pocket a tiny package, all the time smiling at us through tears and gesturing for us to come closer. Cautiously, I took a small step forward. Studying him intently, I watched him peel away some colored paper to reveal a flat piece of shiny silver. Under the foil paper was a grayish-green piece of something. He smiled, and yet he was wiping away tears as if he might be angry.

Slowly, carefully, he placed the mysterious thing between my lips. He did the same to Piet. I said to myself, I'm not going to eat anything you give me. If the Germans didn't poison me, you aren't going to. I promised Martin I would live to get out of this place. Where was Martin? I still couldn't see him. Piet and I stood there, our teeth clenched. The soldier seemed to be looking at us with kindness, but I couldn't be sure. I just looked at him warily, not moving a muscle. Then he unwrapped another piece like the ones he had given us and put it in his own mouth, pointing to his jaw as he made chewing motions. If he would eat it, it must be all right, I thought, so I pushed my piece into my mouth and slowly, intensely, I began to chew. A burst of sweetness filled my mouth, my first taste of something sweet in almost two years. This was good. I had never tasted anything like it before. I smiled at the soldier in return. This was my introduction to the chewing gum the American GIs were famous for.

Something told me I could trust these Americans. I inched closer to the outstretched arms of this soldier with his unknown language and tear-filled eyes. I looked again for Martin in the pandemonium, calling his name, shouting over the din for him to come out from where he was

UPI/Bettmann Newsphotos. Used with permission.

The concentration camp outside of Nordhausen,
Germany, April 1945.

hiding. Again, nothing. I walked into the soldier's arms and felt him embrace me tenderly. I knew nothing about him, not his name, nor his mission. It didn't seem to matter to him that I was caked with filth, that my hair was matted and my clothes reeked from months of living in squalor. I didn't look much better than the wasted corpses littering the camp. I touched his green uniform to make sure it was real, then simply let him hold me. He hugged me so tightly I thought he was going to crush me, all the time wiping tears away from his face, stroking my head, and murmuring soft words to me that I couldn't understand.

I never knew that a grown man could cry. But then, before I came here, I didn't know that men could do the things I had seen them do. I started to cry, too, tears of joy and relief at our long-awaited deliverance. I had lived to the see the day Martin promised would come. We were set free!

I had to wiggle free of the soldier's arms so I could breathe. He held my hands for awhile, just looking at me, then he let go of me and went over to another child. I found Piet and told him, "If we are wrong, if these soldiers are going to take us to another camp to suffer some more, I want you to kill me. Promise me that. I am not going to another camp, you hear me, Piet!" Piet just gazed at me without seeing me, as if he had not heard a word I had said.

I wondered if these new "captors" would order us to get back to work. But those who were not holding children had either begun to explore the camp or were holding the few remaining Nazi guards at gunpoint. Most of the guards and their killer dogs had vanished into thin air. The Americans weren't threatening any of us or barking commands. They were just looking at the things that surrounded them. Some walked over to the open pits filled with corpses. I could tell by the looks on their faces that they could not comprehend what they were seeing.

The Americans entered Nordhausen with no idea of what they would discover. They found hundreds of slave laborers that were almost unrecognizable as human beings. They found the dead lying among the sick and the dying in the same bunks. They found filth and human excrement covering the people and their barracks. No attempt had been made to prevent or slow the disease and gangrene that had spread unchecked among the prisoners. Many of the soldiers were overcome by nausea.

Some of the soldiers gave us chocolate, the only food they had with them, but we threw them up. Our stomachs could not handle rich food.

I think it was the following day when order was restored to the camp. Many American soldiers had gone into the neighboring town of Nordhausen and ordered local citizens out of their homes to help dig graves to bury the dead. As I watched them go about their grisly task, I could tell they hated doing it. Many of the citizens of Nordhausen deny to this day that there was a death camp near their town.

It took several days to take all the living prisoners away. During all this time, despite my searching, I was unable to find Martin. When our turn came to leave, we were loaded into trucks, courteously this time, with plenty of space so we could sit down comfortably on the floor. As the caravan of trucks rolled away from the camp, I recognized the forgotten fragrance of fresh, clean air. I realized how the stench of burning bodies in the ovens and rotting flesh in the pits must have choked the American soldiers. We had been forced to breathe the very air that carried the last traces of our friends, the final fleeting evidence of their fate.

The trucks took us to a makeshift tent hospital set up by the Red Cross. For the first time in twenty months, I was able to wash in something besides my own urine. I felt the wonderful feeling of warm water and soap sliding across my body, soaking off countless layers of grime. I knew the dirt wouldn't all come off with one bath. As the Red Cross nurses helped us clean the rocklike fecal matter off our limbs, they couldn't hide their shock at our condition. As the filth came off, I could see many lice-infested sores.

The nurses tried to feed Piet and me, but we kept throwing up, so they put needles connected to bags of liquid into our arms and fed us through our veins. A few days later we were able to swallow liquid food, and finally could eat solid food again. It felt like a miracle to have someone taking care of us. The hospital beds and blankets felt like clouds. My body was tired, so very tired.

We stayed in the hospital about two weeks. I asked every nurse and doctor, everyone who came into my room, about Martin. I fell asleep every night seeing his face. I awoke each morning to the pain of his absence.

It seemed like thousands and thousands of people rescued from other camps were arriving at the Red Cross tent hospital every day. Even with good care, many were so weak they died just after being freed. I found out it was the U.S. Third Armored Division who had set us free on the fifteenth day of April in 1945. They had found barely 500 survivors, some pulled from between corpses and so weak they had to be carried out. The mastermind behind this genocide, Adolf Hitler, committed suicide on April 30 of the same year. It was hard for me to believe the news. I thought he was too much of a coward to take his own life.

CHAPTER TWENTY

*The children could not forget their histories, of course,
and just because they were forbidden to speak did not
mean that they would not remember.*

DEBORAH DWORK

As we gained strength, Piet and I were anxious to get home and find out if our family was still alive. Once the Americans sorted out who came from where, the soldiers loaded us on a truck with other Dutch kids and sent us to Amsterdam. This was the best truck ride of my life. I was leaving Nordhausen behind me and was surrounded by friendly people. My tears that day sprang from knowing I was saying good-bye forever to the gentle strangers who had rescued me from hell. Before we knew it, Piet and I found ourselves dropped off in one of Amsterdam's town squares, surrounded by the commotion of music, cheering, and dancing crowds. After being handed two small sacks of food, we squeezed our way through the swarm of people and began our walk home.

We walked through the city, pointing and talking about the terrible destruction of so many buildings we remembered. Block after block had been bombed into rubble, and the streets were broken up and full of potholes. But while our proud city was battered and broken, red-white-and-blue Dutch flags hung boldly from the windows of almost every building left standing, and among the ruined buildings people were singing. The mood felt like one of celebration.

"I hope I never see another Nazi soldier as long as I live," I said to Piet, remembering the tramp of Nazi boots down the street we walked along.

"Me neither," Piet answered. "And I don't ever want to hear another bomb drop over our heads," he said as he gazed into the delft blue sky.

"Do you think Ma and Pa made it through the war?" I asked. It was something we hadn't talked about much at the camp.

"It would take a miracle," Piet said doubtfully.

"I'll bet Ma made it. She's a tough one," I said, only half believing my words.

Just a few more steps and we would be on our own street, the street I hadn't seen since I met Henny and Jenny on that fateful night. Neighbors were hanging out of their windows, but they couldn't tell who we were. As I stepped up to our front door, the first thing I saw was the sign from the Board of Health that had been there all my life. But our shabby little house looked like heaven to me. From the house next door, the Woodpecker leaned forward out of her window, screeching down to us, "Cato, is that you?"

"It sure is," I called back. "Is my mother home?"

But she didn't answer us. She just started shrieking, "Hey! Piet and Cato are home! Piet and Cato are home!" Neighbors came pouring out of their houses like ants scurrying out of the anthills I used to kick in the park. They surrounded us, peppering us with questions: Where have you two been? Are you all right? Did you know your parents thought you were dead? No one listened to our answers. When we tried to ask about our folks, no one could hear us over the talk. Finally, someone told us Pa was home from the war in Germany but not at the house. Ma was at some kind of meeting. Derk, who had married just two days before he was picked up by the Germans, was at Annie's house. The Woodpecker opened our front door and sure enough, the house was a mess.

"Same old place, Cato," Piet sighed.

"I don't care," I replied. "I just hope Pa isn't drinking like he used to."

As we came back outside, everyone was still there, begging to know about the camp, but we told them we would tell them after we found Ma and Pa. The Woodpecker walked us to some kind of class or meeting where Ma was. We knew her from the back because of her hair and familiar dress. The speaker caught sight of us and stopped dead in the middle of a sentence, her mouth hanging open. "Tina," she said in shock, probably wondering if she was seeing two ghosts, "your son and daughter are here." She dropped to a chair, and Ma stood up and turned around. She looked at us and fell to the floor in a dead faint. We rushed over to fan her face, and when she opened her eyes, they welled up with tears.

"Cato! Piet! Cato! Piet!" she cried hysterically, "We thought you were dead." As she sat up, we fell into her arms and helped her cry. Walking toward home in the bombed out streets, we told her what we had been through for so many months.

"I just can't believe it," she said. "But then looking at how awful the two of you look, I can believe it. You look like skeletons! Didn't the Germans feed you?"

"Not really, Ma. What they gave us you couldn't really call food." Piet said, gagging at the memory.

"Well, both of you look like hell," she muttered.

Ma looked older, thinner, and more slumped over than I remembered. How had she felt when she thought we were dead? I wished I had been around to see how long she cried. What about Pa? Before I could ask, Ma asked, "Do you remember where the bar is, Piet?"

"Of course I do," he replied sadly, "But I'm not going down there."

So she sent the Woodpecker, who was still fluttering around us in amazement. Now came my chance to ask the question that had been on my mind every day for nearly twenty months. "Ma, have you seen Henny and Jenny?"

"No, Cato, we haven't seen them for over a year. Their father got killed by a sniper."

"Good," I said vindictively.

As we sat down in the living room, I remembered the night of the bombing, the shattered glass, and the terror. I had seen so much worse since then, it seemed like nothing. Mollie, my cat, was still frightfully thin, but alive. Pa burst through the door, shouting, "Piet, Cato, we thought you were dead!" He picked us both up, one under each arm, and swung us around. His breath reeked of alcohol, but his smile spoke pure joy. "You two are skin and bones." He set us down and felt our scrawny arms. "Now sit down and tell us the whole story." I sat on his lap, amid memories of old fears. Piet and I took turns telling them everything—about the party, the boat, the misery, hunger, torture, and deaths. And, of course, Martin. They seemed to sink lower and lower in their chairs as they listened to our nightmarish tale, their expressions changing from disbelief to sorrow to rage.

"It is amazing you two are still alive," Pa said, hugging us again.

"Well, Pa," Piet said softly, "I don't think we could have made it much longer."

Rubbing our heads affectionately, Pa took a closer look. "You have sores worse than ever!"

"They used to be a lot worse, Pa, believe me. The Red Cross ladies took care of them while we were in the hospital, but there still must be lice in them, because they itch a lot," I said.

"Well, we better get them out now, so they don't get in your beds."

So our welcome home was sitting still while Pa shaved off all our hair and wrapped our heads in petrol-soaked rags. I didn't mind him shaving our heads—what hair we had wasn't much to look at. He spent hours digging out lice and their nests from our raw sores. It hurt, of course, and we lost a lot of blood, but I was so accustomed to pain, I hardly winced.

The real pain came with what Pa did next. He sat us down and said, "Now kids, I know you had a terrible time in the camp, but you must now put it out of your minds and never talk about it again."

"But, Pa," we protested, our words tumbling over each other.

"We need to tell someone!" Piet insisted. "We can't just forget a year and a half of hell that easy."

"Your Pa is right," Ma interrupted. "I don't want you to ever talk about it again. It's in the past now."

I couldn't believe this. "But Pa, Ma," I argued passionately, "I can still see the dead bodies rotting around us. Every time I close my eyes, I can still see and taste the maggots I had to eat. I've got to talk to someone. I can't understand all the cruel things they did."

But Pa was adamant. "I won't hear another word about it, do you hear me?" he demanded, the old fierceness creeping into his voice. Piet and I looked at each other in silent amazement. We had not expected this. "Sure," we agreed reluctantly, "we won't talk about it."

The nightmares began that night.

CHAPTER TWENTY-ONE

*My nightmares will continue to haunt me as long as I
live for it is then that I see everyone as I knew them in
their pure and noble lives, and as I saw them oppressed
till they were like dust.*

SARA ZYSKIND

I didn't care what my father said, I had to talk to someone. The next day I ran to Greet's house, my bald head covered by a scarf. We cried in each other's arms. She, too, had assumed I was dead. Her body had grown, while mine had seemed to shrink. She was even taller, and her blonde hair was long, though she was still rail-thin from the years of hunger. After telling her about our ordeal, Pa's demand for silence, and the nightmares, she came up with an idea. Good old Greet, still full of ideas.

"Why don't you talk to Mr. Speets about it, Cato?" she suggested.

"Is he still around?" I asked. "Didn't he have to fight in the war?"

"No, he was one of the lucky ones, I guess. After you were taken, it got to be real bad. Those lousy Nazis were going around in their jackass trucks, picking up anyone, not just Jews. A lot of people went to the so-called work camps."

We talked about everything, about my life and hers since being separated. She told me nobody had tried to help Sonja walk since I left, they were too worried about staying alive. I told her about Martin. I told her that I had changed my mind about being a doctor. I now wanted to be a nurse, Martin's nurse. I still hoped I could find him.

"Cato, it costs a lot of money to become a nurse," Greet warned.

"I know, but I'm going to find a way, no matter what." I knew I had to do more than just survive in this world.

The walk to Sonja's house with Greet was filled with both gratitude and disappointment. I was home, but Amsterdam was in shambles. Greet and Sonja were still here, but Henny and Jenny were nowhere to be found. My beloved canal was smellier than ever, and yet sweetly fragrant to me. At least it was the smell of life, not death. I wanted to jump right in, but my head still throbbed from the lice harvest, and I had finally learned some restraint.

Sonja seemed so happy to see me, but as we talked, I sensed she was depressed. Perhaps I reminded her of the hope she had once had of walking. When she told me she had given up on ever walking because of what a doctor had told her, I was furious.

"Sonja, now that the war is over, we are going to take you anywhere and everywhere we go. You're going to walk, run, and dance, you just watch," I promised.

"No. Thank you for saying that, but I'm not going to fool myself anymore," she said tearfully. "I'm so much trouble to everybody, I wish my mother had killed me when she tried."

I couldn't bear to see her cry. She reminded me of when Piet had given up.

"Sonja! How do you know your mother tried to kill you before you were born?" I pressed her.

"She has told me over and over that she wished I hadn't been born." Sonja sobbed. I wondered if the strains of war had made Sonja's mother crazy.

"To want to kill a baby," Greet whispered. "That's disgusting." I didn't tell her what it reminded me of.

At home, nothing had changed. Piet kept everything inside himself. He went off with his friend, Bertus, almost every day and was seldom at home. Derk had come home badly burned from an explosion. Annie's mother took care of him at her house, and he never came to visit. Pa was drinking an awful lot, Ma was the same housekeeper she had always been. For me, the nightmares seemed to be getting more frequent. I always dreamed the same thing. I saw a circle of skeletons dancing around a deep hole filled with stacks of bodies. I was holding hands with the skeletons. I knew I had do something. I was fourteen years old, living in a child's body with the mind of an adult.

Pa made Piet and me go back to school, even though I did not like going with sores all over my body. After a few weeks, I found Mr. Speets, who was teaching younger children. He looked up in surprise and smiled. "It is so good to see you again, Cato," he said warmly. Tears trickled down my cheeks.

"What's happening, Cato?" he asked. "I know you and your brother went through a terrible ordeal. Do you want to sit down and talk to me?" He pulled up another chair and I sat down next to his desk. I felt deep down inside that if he had been my father, my life would have been so different.

"It's a very long story. Do you think I could come back another time and tell you about it? Do you have time?" I asked.

"I'll always make time for you. Why don't you start right now?" But I didn't know where to start, and I just sat there weeping.

Mr. Speets said tenderly, "Cato, ever since you came back to school, you've looked so different, so serious. I think you are carrying quite a load in that little heart of yours. Is that why you came to see me?"

"Oh, Mr. Speets, my parents won't let me talk about it, and I'm afraid if I don't talk with someone, I'm going to explode. I'm afraid to go to sleep at night because of my horrible nightmares."

"Was it that bad, Cato?" he asked.

Wiping my tears off my face, I answered, "I want to go home now, but is it all right if I come and talk to you tomorrow?"

"Of course it is, Cato," he reassured me.

Mollie was the only one home when I got there. She curled up in my lap as I sat in the corner of the living room, thinking. No one seemed to be able to understand what Nordhausen was really like. Some people refused to believe it was as bad as I said. At least Mollie wouldn't tell me to be quiet. Even Sonja was telling me to forget what had happened. How did she think I could forget? She told me I sounded so grown-up. I knew that I would never be a child again. If only I had Martin to talk to—he would understand.

After school the next day, Mr. Speets was sitting at his desk grading papers when I came in. I sat on a chair close to him, and we talked about everything. He wanted to tell me some things about Adolf Hitler to help me understand what a sick man he was. "Did the Jews ever do anything to make him hate them like he did?" I asked.

"I don't know," he said. "Some people who knew him when he was younger thought he was mentally ill. But there was something in his eyes and the way he spoke that drew people to him. And some people say he had Jewish blood in him."

I didn't want to talk about Hitler, but Mr. Speets thought it would help. I wanted to talk about what Hitler had done to my life, how he had changed it forever. We talked more about the camp and before I left, he asked if Piet would like to come and visit him, too.

I began seeing Mr. Speets regularly, but it took me a few weeks to talk Piet into coming with me. I was getting worried about my brother. He hardly spoke to me. Even though we had suffered together, I felt that I understood him less than I understood anyone.

Piet said to me one day, "I heard you screaming and whimpering in your sleep the other night, Cato. Was it real bad?" His brow was wrinkled and he looked serious beyond his years. I had hoped no one had heard me.

"Yes, it was terrible, but no worse than any of the other nights. I could see the Nazis leading all those people to the showers and hear the screaming and clawing sounds. I felt myself holding hands with corpses." I shivered. "How about you?"

"I dream about those things, too. I keep seeing the faces of the corpses and the blood," he said somberly. "It feels like the burning smell penetrated my skin and I can't get it out." It was about then he decided to come with me to see Mr. Speets.

The first time he came, talking about his memories rekindled all his fury. "Listen here, Mr. Speets, you won't know how terrible it really was until you've spent day after day, week after week, month after month in a place like that," he raged. "It doesn't help to talk about it; I'm just making myself mad!"

He shook Mr. Speets's hand. "Thank you for trying, but I have to go." Piet turned and trudged out, his shoulders sagging.

"I'm sorry, Mr. Speets," I said dismally.

"I think he'll come back, Cato. He just needs a little time. Maybe it's because he's older than you," he said. I stayed a long time that afternoon.

After a few weeks, Piet tried again. Always, my teacher listened patiently, crying along with us when the details overcame him, encouraging us to begin to forgive. He said, "Maybe you will never forget, and there may be some people in camp who were so cruel, you can't forgive them. But I want you to try. I know you never had it easy at home and then you ended up in a camp that was even worse. Try not to let it fester in your mind." He told me—and I think he truly believed it—that my life would get better. Mr. Speets gave us what Martin had given—comfort and hope. I tried to hang on to those fragile feelings while I watched Ma and Pa curse at each other and throw things. I practiced what I had discovered in the camp—that if I put things out of my mind and thought of something else, I could endure just about anything.

I unburdened my heart to Mr. Speets on many, many afternoons. Piet quit going, choosing to keep it all blocked inside himself. He was cut from a different pile of wood than I was, I guess.

Going back to school helped me as I tried to get to a point where I felt normal again. I wanted part of my childhood back, and my Dutch stubbornness helped me to get some of it. Greet helped me laugh again as we went to dances and carnivals and skated on the canal. We played new tricks and kept an eye out for boys. Still I felt like an adult trapped inside a child's body.

~·~··~··~··~··~·~

CHAPTER TWENTY TWO

To live authentically in [the Holocaust's] aftermath,
one must be aware of the reality of radical evil and its
startling triumphs, and I fight against that evil and that
triumph.

MICHAEL BERENBAUM

Pa kept mentioning to me that he had a friend who wanted me to come to work in his leather factory. I knew better and boldly let him know that I had other plans. However, the spring I turned sixteen, I found Pa at home one afternoon, stone sober for a change. "Cato," he announced, "I have spoken again to my friend who owns the leather factory." I didn't say anything. "He says he would like you to come by the factory on Saturday, and he will tell you all about the job and will start paying you as soon as you start."

"Pa," I said, "Don't you remember, I'm going to be a nurse. I want to help people."

He raised his voice. "I've told you over and over again that being a nurse is a dirty job. You have to wash people, empty bedpans, and do all sorts of other things."

"But Pa, someone has do it," I shrugged, "and it might as well be me."

"Well, that someone is not going to be you," he snapped. How many times did we have to go through this? Knowing Pa wouldn't back down, I offered a compromise.

"Pa, I'll make a deal with you. I'll work in your friend's factory for one year, and if I like it I'll stay. But if I don't like it, you let me become a nurse. How about it?"

He didn't even think about it, just answered doubtfully, "We'll have to see, Cato. But it is important that you see this man on Saturday, okay?"

"Oh, all right, Pa," I agreed sadly.

Dutifully, I kept my Saturday appointment at the leather factory and told the owner right off that I didn't want to make purses. I told him I didn't even care how much I got paid because I had to give most of the money to my mother who would just waste it on cakes for her friends. He hired me anyway and I started working there halfheartedly as soon as school was out, stuck at a machine all day sewing handles on handbags. I hated every minute of it. I kept hoping my folks would see how unhappy I was and would let me learn to be a nurse.

The year went by surprisingly fast, and then I had to wait a few weeks for an evening when my father was sober. I had to be very careful that I didn't set off his temper. I sat down across the kitchen table from him and began in my calmest voice, "Pa, do you remember how I said I would work in the leather factory for one year and see if I liked it." He already looked suspicious. "Well," I continued, "I've given this job a whole year, and I've decided I'm ready to become a nurse now."

Pa bolted upright, almost tipping over his chair. "Cato, I don't want you to be a nurse and I've never wanted you to be one," he roared. "I will not discuss this again."

I jumped up, shouting, "Pa, you're not being fair about this. I hate the factory! I hate leather!"

"That's too bad, Cato. You're not going to be a nurse, and that's final." I left before I could see if he reached for one of his bottles of whiskey. I rode my bicycle furiously to Greet's house.

"Oh, Greet," I seethed, "Pa won't let me quit working at the factory. I thought after a year he would listen to me."

"Did you tell him how boring it is and how much you hate it?" Greet questioned.

"Of course I did. He doesn't care if I am happy or not," I said. It stung to pronounce the truth I had known all my life.

"You're not going to give up your dream, are you?"

I had spent months fighting for my physical life. I had barely survived, and now it felt like Pa was trying to kill my soul. "No," I declared. "I'm not giving up."

"What are you going to do.?

"Well, I guess it's simple. I'll just have to run away. I can't stay with Pa anyway. He's worse than ever." I didn't have to tell Greet what I meant.

"The cops would have you back as soon as you left," she warned.

"Not if I find someplace to hide." What Pa didn't realize is that I was not the Cato he had known. I had lived from one hellish minute to the next longing only for freedom, witnessing hundreds of lives destroyed. Pa would not destroy mine now.

Greet pleaded with me, "Please Cato, don't run away. I'll ask my folks if you can stay with us."

I hated work more every day. I daydreamed about helping the sick while I tied leather cords on one purse after another. I was so bored I could have screamed. Meanwhile, things were getting worse at home. Many times as I left for work in the morning I had to step over Pa asleep at the bottom of the stairs.

One day Greet told me that her parents felt it would be a good idea for me to stay with them while I applied for nurse's training. Suddenly it wasn't such a simple decision. As shaky as it was, the security I had with my parents was strong enough to make me stop and think. Should I burn a bridge behind me for a future that might not work out the way I planned? I thought about my decision as I worked, going back and forth in my feelings.

A few weeks later, just before quitting time, I was thinking about everything I dreaded going home to, and without warning, my decision was made. It came with such finality, I slammed the purse I was working on down on the table. My co-workers looked at me with startled expressions. I felt my whole body tighten with determination. I went straight home from work and packed my few worn-out clothes in my old schoolbag. Then I rode over to Greet's to tell her parents I was ready to leave home. They asked me to promise I would not tell my parents where I was.

Every purse I touched the next day reminded me that this part of my life was over. I don't remember thinking once about how my folks would feel if I left. That night I excused myself after dinner, telling my parents I was not feeling well. It was the truth—my stomach was knotted with fear. I lay on my bed about an hour, and then I made my move. I sneaked downstairs, bag in hand, as if tip-toeing through glass. Just as I stepped down the last step, Ma came out of the living room on her way to the bathroom. She pushed the glasses back on her nose and cocked her head to one side suspiciously.

"I'm feeling a lot better, Ma, and I thought I'd go over to show Sonja something." I smiled.

"What's in your bag?" she probed, reaching for it.

"Oh, just some things I want to show her." I held the bag close to me and stepped around her toward the front door.

Narrowing her eyes, she said, "Just be back in half an hour."

I was on my bike and on my way when Pa came out the door, weaving slightly and calling for me to come back. When I didn't stop, I heard his angry voice call, "Cato, get back home this minute." Over my shoulder, I could see him pedaling after me on his bike and knew I should have waited until he was too drunk to follow me. Ahead of me I could see the street that ran alongside one of the city's major canals, and I realized he was getting closer. Turning at the corner, I was momentarily out of his sight.

Fear pounded like a hammer against my ribs. Riding parallel to the canal, I could see the moonlight reflecting off the slow water. A crazy idea hit me—since I knew the canal so well, why not go in bike and all? A quick glance told me Pa hadn't reached this street yet, but I had to hurry. I made a sharp right turn, and for an instant was in midair. Then

I was suddenly surrounded by the black slimy water of the canal. I could feel the slippery, slanted concrete bank under me. Trying to keep my footing and knowing the canal was overrun by rats this time of the year, I fought to hold on to the bike. I was willing to risk drowning to get a better life for myself. I had lived long enough in places that did not make me happy.

Thinking Pa had passed me, I dragged the bike up on the grassy part of the bank. I could see him up ahead, slowing down, then stopping and looking around. I rolled my bike right back down into the canal, took an enormous gulp of air, and pulled my head under the murky water. I stayed under until I thought my lungs would burst, and when I came up, he was gone. I got even dirtier dragging my bike up the bank and back to the street. The closest place I could go in my dripping, smelly clothes was Derk and Annie's house. When they asked me in surprise why I was so wet, I cried, "Pa is after me. I ran away from home and had to ride into the canal to hide from Pa."

Derk wrapped me in a blanket and in his love. "Oh, Cato, you and your crazy ideas." I sat with them until I was warm and almost dry. Derk asked, "So where do you think Pa went after you fell into the canal?"

"I didn't fall in, I rode in!" I said. He grimaced at the thought of anyone intentionally going into that filthy ditch. "Pa probably went to Sonja or Greet's house."

There was a thunderous pounding at the door, and Annie slipped me into a back room as Pa stormed past Derk and into the kitchen. I heard his enraged voice saying, "I know your sister is here because her bicycle is right outside your door, so where is she? She lied that she was going to see that crippled friend of hers." His voice became a mumble as they closed the kitchen door. I slipped down the hall to the front door. Quickly I rode to Greet's where her kind parents hid my bike and spent the next few hours calming me down. Greet's father took me to the police station the following morning to get permission to have me stay with them, then he told me, "I admire you for your determination to be a nurse, Cato, and we will try to help you. But you have to promise me that you will someday make friends again with your parents."

"I'll see," I answered. "But first let me enroll in nursing school." Why make a promise I'd never keep?

After the best night's sleep I'd had in years, I walked with Greet and her father to the hospital so I could talk to the administrator. What if this stranger brought my dream to an abrupt end? Each step took me closer to that possibility. What would I do? The man told me that the training would be very difficult, that I would spend the first six weeks without any contact with patients, going to class during the day and scrubbing floors and bedpans in the evenings. I nervously told him that I was willing and waited for his response. With little deliberation he accepted me and assigned me a room in the nurses' dormitory. Greet and her father may have walked home on the sidewalk, but as for me, I felt like I was flying.

After we passed our first exams at the end of six weeks, the hospital issued us each a blue dress with a white apron and stiffly starched cuffs, a veil, and black shoes and stockings. We all looked like Florence Nightingale. Each week the training became more challenging, with every night spent studying with the other students. Saturdays were for visiting families, but I knew my parents would not want to see me.

It took almost five months before I decided to go home for a visit. As suddenly as I had known I would run away, I decided it was time to try to make peace. It must have been related to my feeling that I was succeeding at something important. I got all dressed up in my nice new uniform and went to see Ma and Pa. Ma greeted me with a smirk and a sarcastic, "Well, how about that? The long lost daughter is coming home. Don't you look fancy!" She threw in a few choice cuss words for spice.

I stayed calm, a grand accomplishment for me. "Mother," I said, "Let's stop right there. Let's just be friends."

"Well, come in then," Ma said wearily, "But I warn you, your father is drunk." What's new about that, I thought.

Pa sat in his same old place at the table, his row of whiskey bottles at his feet. He looked up at me with glassy eyes. "What the hell are you doing here?" he slurred.

"Shut up, Gerard," Ma snapped. "She's a nurse and she came home to visit, so behave yourself."

"So you finally did it, didn't you, Cato?" he taunted in a cold, accusing tone of voice. "You couldn't stay at the factory and learn a good trade. And now you want us to take you back in the house?"

"No, Pa. I live at the hospital. Nurse's training is very hard work, but I love it. We had a little free time, so I thought I should come and see you."

"Well," my father retorted, "you needn't have bothered for us."

"Please, Pa," I begged. "If you will treat me with respect, we can be friends. If you don't want that, I won't bother coming back."

"Ain't she miss uppity," Ma sneered.

"Never mind. I need to get back to the hospital," I said, turning to leave.

As I took hold of the doorknob, I heard Pa say in a voice so soft I almost didn't hear him, "Cato." I turned around to see him stand and steady himself. He looked directly into my eyes and said in an earnest, subdued voice, "Don't leave. We want to be friends. Will you stay and have a cup of coffee with us before you go?" For over an hour we sat and talked as friends.

And so it was that, eighteen years after I was born, I at last felt welcomed in my home.

CHAPTER TWENTY-THREE

*Whoever is happy will make others happy too. He who
has courage and faith will never perish in misery!*

ANNE FRANK

Our first year exam consisted of going alone before a panel of six doctors and the director of the hospital and answering questions so difficult I was afraid I would fail. The announcement was made two days later that only two students had failed, and I wasn't one of them!

Conversations about people who had immigrated to other countries became commonplace among the nurses. Their stories intrigued me and I longed to know more. I couldn't forget the first Americans I had seen at Nordhausen, so gentle and caring. Since then, Greet and I had met a few who had "invaded" the local Saturday night dances with their laughter and charm. They sure seemed to know how to have a good time.

Out of curiosity, I went to our capital city, The Hague, to ask about moving to America. I found out that even if I filled out papers that day, it may take five years to move to the top of the waiting list. What can I lose, I thought. So I quickly filled out all the papers right then. As the months and then years of waiting passed, I tried to pick up a little English by watching American movies, but I had to read the Dutch subtitles to really understand what was being said.

After I had become a registered nurse and had been working at the hospital awhile, I began to wonder where my name was on the waiting list for America. When I rode my bike over to the office in The Hague, a man checked the files and told me the papers had been sent to me about a year before. I asked him how that could possibly be because I still lived and worked at the same hospital. As he pointed out to me the address I had written down, my knees almost buckled as the awful realization hit me—I had put down my parents' address!

I had never told my folks about my desire to leave Holland. During my occasional visits, I carefully avoided the subject, knowing they would hate the idea. Now I pedaled frantically to their home. The house was filled with Ma's gossiping friends, nibbling on cake and sipping coffee.

Winded and panting, I confronted her in front of her friends. "Ma, did some papers come for me from The Hague about a year ago that you never told me about?" I demanded. She opened any mail that came for me.

With a look of total innocence, she glanced up from her cake and said, "I didn't see any." I left in a huff.

Later that evening, I rode back and questioned Ma and Pa together. This time Pa reluctantly admitted that they couldn't bear to see me leave Holland. So they had thrown my papers in the fire.

"You did what?" I hollered. "You had absolutely no right to do that!"

My mother hollered right back, "You don't know anything about the country you think you are going to. You don't even speak English!" Then in a quieter voice, tinged with regret, she continued, "You'll be moving away from here and we might never see you again."

I flew into a rage. "I don't care if I ever see either of you again. You had no right to ruin my future. You've never done anything to make life easy for me. Thanks a lot for ruining it again!" I slammed the door so hard I thought the house would tumble down.

I called the consulate at The Hague early the next morning, but an official told me I would have to start all over again—apply and wait five years. I wanted to scream, but who was there to hear?

I tried to think of someone who might be able to help me. The most important man I knew was the director of the hospital. When I told him of my terrible disappointment, he pledged to see if he could help. A week later he called me into his office and explained another way to get to America. It was longer and more round about, but it was a way. In a few short months, I could immigrate to Canada.

"It is a big decision, Cato," he cautioned. "The only help you would have would be a good-bye and a pat on the back. Whatever happens there would be entirely up to you. Canada is beautiful, but the winters are bad."

I didn't need to think about it. "Then that is what I want to do," I told him.

He took my hand. "Cato, I know with what you have been through, you're tough enough to make it, but you'll always have a job here if things don't work out," he promised.

"Thank you for your confidence in me, sir," I said.

The movies I saw at the Canadian consulate left me thinking that the whole country was filled with cowboys who rode horses and struck matches on the soles of their boots. After my physical examination I felt like a horse myself, as the doctor looked me over, poking and prodding me until I was sore. For the trip I purchased the most enormous suitcase I could find. It was so huge, I could curl up in it myself. Sonja and Greet came to the hospital while I was packing my clothes, and they teased me, saying my suitcase was big enough to use for a bedroom.

"Did you know that they still ride horses in Canada? When they ride up to a building, they tie their horses on a post outside, and they carry guns. Maybe you'll see me riding a horse in my nurse's uniform with a gun at my side," I chuckled.

Sonja made a face. "Do they really still do that?" she asked.

"That's what the movies show," I said.

My last visit with my folks was very short. I told them I was leaving for Canada the next day and when and where the ship embarked. They were offended, but I wouldn't let that change my mind. "Why didn't you tell us sooner?" my mother asked.

"Because I didn't want you to wreck it for me like you did the last

Cato, shortly after nurses' training.

time," I explained. It was easier than saying farewell to the nurses at the Red Cross hospital had been. No hugs, no tears—just good-bye, good luck, and I was gone. It was harder with Annie and Derk. I couldn't find Piet.

Ma and Pa did not show up to see me off, but all my friends did, and we cried freely. As Holland disappeared beyond the horizon, my tears dried, and I settled into my small cabin. My nightmares had also faded away, as Mr. Speets had hoped, unless someone asked me too many questions about Nordhausen. It was early spring, 1954. I was almost twenty-three years old.

When the ship docked in Halifax, Nova Scotia, ten days later, I saw a crowd along the deck. I remarked to a fellow at my side that I didn't see any horses like they had in the movies. But the cars—I had never seen so many cars.

"They don't ride horses anymore except on the farms," the man told me.

"What about the movies?" I asked.

"Ah," he said. "Those movies are really old."

I felt silly, but soon forgot about it as I stood in line for hours to be processed through customs. After my clumsy luggage and I finally passed inspection, I was told I could have a train ticket to wherever I wanted to go.

"One place is as good as another to me," I told the ticket agent.

He looked at me like I was crazy, but a man behind me spoke up in a strange combination of Dutch and English. "Sir, give her a ticket to Toronto. I'm from Holland. My family is going there. We can help her out along the way."

So with thirty Canadian dollars in my pocket, a suitcase almost as big as I was, new traveling companions, and a dream, I began the three-day train trip to Toronto. I almost got back off the train when I saw that instead of wide comfortable seats, we had wooden slats to sit on. We were each given a pillow and blanket and we had to make the best of it.

Massive mountains and miles of snowy evergreens passed by as the train went on and on. Coming from crowded little Holland, I couldn't fathom the size of this country. "What's Toronto like?" I asked the Dutchman who had offered to help me.

"It is a very large city," he said. "At least I think so."

"You mean to tell me you've never been there, either?" I gasped. "You've been talking like you are from there."

"No," he explained. "I wrote letters for years to a friend who lives there. That's who my family is going to stay with for awhile."

"Is it always so cold?" I asked.

"Cold?" the man laughed. "They told me this is a lot warmer than it was last month. Sometimes it gets down to 50 degrees below zero here."

The towering buildings of Toronto made me feel very small. When we got off the train, the man and his family told me good-bye and wished me the best. "Does this mean you're going to leave me?" I asked, stunned.

"I'm sorry, we can't help you any further. But you're in Toronto and you can go to the Dutch consulate. Tell them you are here without friends or relatives and can speak no English." I was so downhearted I forgot to ask him where the Dutch consulate was.

In my light coat, nylons, and high heels, I was chilled to the bone and couldn't stop shaking. I started walking aimlessly, lugging a suitcase that felt as though it were filled with rocks. I walked and walked, not knowing where I was going, wandering further into the heart of the city. Before I knew it, the sun had gone down and I had come to a park. I was utterly alone. I brushed snow off a bench and sat down sobbing, my tears freezing on my face. How stupid I had been to come without knowing how to speak English. I had no idea how far thirty dollars would go. Would it even buy me dinner?

I had never prayed in my life, but at that moment I knew I would freeze to death if I didn't get help. Silently, I pled with Oma's God.

A ridiculous idea came into my head, but I was so cold I didn't care. I took a few things out of my trunk, placed them under the bench, and curled up between my uniforms inside it. Although its snugness cramped me, once I closed the lid the suitcase was quickly warmed by my body heat. Memories raced through my head, but the thing that struck me most was what Sonja had told me in Holland—that my trunk was big enough for me to use as a bedroom. She was right. I drifted into a fitful sleep.

For two more nights and two days, I stayed in the park, nibbling on the last candy bars I had brought from home and quenching my thirst with snow. My body recognized the tired, cold, and hunger of Nordhausen. Fearful of starving, I knew I had to do something quickly. I repacked my things and went looking for a train station so I could go back to Halifax and on to Holland. People stared at me, a young girl lugging a huge trunk with tears streaming down her face, but no one stopped to help.

Again I prayed, hoping it might work again, while I wandered by several restaurants, afraid to go in for fear I didn't have enough money. Then I heard it. Someone called my name. "Cato! Cato! Is that you?" I saw a young fellow running towards me waving his arms. Then I grinned.

It was Wayne, a Canadian soldier I had met briefly in Amsterdam while he was in the hospital for appendicitis. He spoke quite good Dutch and had been great fun to talk to. This was good fortune beyond anything I could have imagined.

"I can't believe it's you, Wayne." I cried, throwing my arms around his neck.

"How did you get here?" he asked, looking at me in awe.

Weak from hunger and relief, I told him about the trip and the nights in my trunk, my meals of chocolate and water. I found out he was staying with friends in Toronto before moving to the United States. "It's good to see you haven't lost your spirit, Cato," he laughed. He bought me a steak so big I thought he had ordered the whole cow. In the warm comfort of the restaurant over dinner, he shocked me with the suggestion that I marry him so I could go with him to the U.S. When I laughed it off, he offered to take me in his car to his friend's house and see if I could stay with them for awhile.

"You have a car?" I was dumbstruck.

"Of course. Everyone has a car here." I decided not to mention the horses.

Wayne's friends were kind enough to take me in in exchange for helping with their children, and when he left a few days later, he made another offer to marry me. I told him I had to make it on my own first and not go to the States through someone else. I thanked him for taking care of me, knowing that I might have died without him.

"No, Cato," he smiled, "You would never have died. You're too stubborn for that. Good luck, kid, I love you." And he was gone.

I picked up a few English words, enough so I could find my way home when I was lost. I found work in a nursing home, but I wanted to nurse people back to good health, not take care of them until they died. A Dutch gentleman I met offered to help me find a better job, and when he did, I unexpectedly found a family, too. Acting as my interpreter, he helped me apply for a job with Marion Cox and her parents, Harold and Eva. Marion was a young woman who needed someone to care for her mother and grandmother, who were both ill. They lived in Orillia, Ontario, Canada, a small town at that time. Although we couldn't understand each other, I could tell they were good, kind people and I fell in love with them at once. I was tickled to have a room all to myself. The family's compassion was evident in the way they treated the sick. They had even rigged a series of mirrors so the grandmother, bedfast with a broken hip, could see what was happening in the living room. We communicated with a Dutch-English dictionary and sign language.

Gradually the dictionary lay unopened more and more often. Marion and I joined a bowling team and loved our nights out. I grew close enough to Marion's parents to call them Mom and Pop. At one of our get-togethers with a family who lived by a lake, I was offered my first alcoholic drink, blackberry wine. Even though I remembered Pa's problem, I took a delicious sip. Within half an hour, I had downed the whole bottle and was so drunk I could hardly walk. I got an idea in my head to get into a boat, but I made it rock so hard I fell like a sack of potatoes and cut my jaw badly. Marion drove me back to the house with one hand on the steering wheel and the other keeping me from jumping out of the pickup so I could throw up. I made her promise not to tell anyone I had guzzled the whole bottle of wine. She thought it was funny, but the whole thing reminded me too much of what I had left back in Holland, and I resolved never to let myself get in that condition again.

One night, Marion asked me to accompany her to the library, and after about an hour I was peeved at myself for wasting so much time there. We came home to a dark house, and I tiptoed into the living room. "SURPRISE!" twenty voices shouted, as the lights flashed on and twenty beaming faces surrounded me. The whole bowling team was there. Marion took an envelope from her mother and presented me with a round-trip ticket to Holland. I couldn't see my other presents for the tears, but they included a camera, and several new suitcases—too small to sleep in, my friends teased. It wasn't my birthday or an anniversary or anything, simply a kind gesture of friendship, appreciated more deeply than I could tell them.

I found so much had changed in Amsterdam when I returned. The bombed out buildings had been rebuilt. Piet was married, but seemed aloof and unconcerned that I was around. The hospital director had passed away. Even the hospital looked different. Greet had immigrated to Australia; I couldn't find Sonja. Yet so much had stayed the same. My parents' house was the same as when I left—chaotic, contentious, lonely. I spent several days touring and talking with Annie and Derk, then began to feel the tug of homesickness for my new land. I knew it was time to return.

Getting back to Canada was like coming home. Not long after my return, my friends gave me a beat-up 1938 Plymouth that smoked like crazy if I went over forty-five miles per hour. I stuffed the dented fender with rags that came tumbling out every few potholes. All I had ever owned was a bike, so I was glad to travel with a roof overhead. Once, as I drove along with a backseat stuffed with three guys and three girl-friends squeezed in the front, a cop pulled me over for going too fast through town.

"Don't worry, boys," I crowed to my male cargo. "You just keep quiet and I'll pretend that we're all Dutch and can't understand what he says." The officer sauntered up to my jalopy. Rolling down the window,

I gave him the most cheerful Dutch greeting I could think of. Without missing a beat, he replied in perfect Dutch and wrote out the ticket. I fumed as my friends in the back were dying from laughter.

Those were heady, happy days—surrounded by people who loved me as I loved them, free to get around in a car, doing the things I enjoyed most.

CHAPTER TWENTY-FOUR

It wasn't the ruthlessness that enabled an individual to
survive. It was an intangible quality . . . an overriding
thirst . . . perhaps, too, a talent for life, and a faith in life.

DEATH CAMP SURVIVOR

(QUOTED BY TERRENCE DES PRES IN

THE WORLD MUST KNOW)

A correspondence with a man in British Columbia, three thousand miles away, set me thinking about a move. I felt it was time for a change, so I moved to Canada's Pacific coast and easily found work in a Catholic hospital that treated patients with multiple sclerosis. Though I could do little to ease the pain and sorrow of the patients suffering from this terminal illness, I did what I could. Ever so often, I wished for Martin to see me doing such important work. I wondered if someone somewhere was being comforted by his tender hand, as I had been.

About this time I began writing to an American who was in the Air Force. For his vacation, he followed his letters to British Columbia and we dated for several weeks. When he proposed marriage, I accepted. I knew very little about him, but I did know that I was terribly lonely. He must have been lonely too—he had grown up in an orphanage. We were married in front of a justice of the peace, and a week later he returned to his base in Florida. As a Canadian citizen, I had to stay behind and wait for him to send immigration papers.

When I did move to Florida to be with him three months later, I discovered I was pregnant. I was happier than I had ever been, or so I thought. But I began to notice little things about my husband's behavior that didn't seem quite right. I was used to being around friends and co-workers who could work out problems on their own, but he had real difficulty dealing with everyday things.

The birth of my first son filled me with immeasurable joy. He was perfectly formed, but so tiny I could scarcely believe he would grow up to be a man. We called him Johnny. My happiness wouldn't last. Shortly after Johnny's birth, a doctor gravely told me that Johnny had cerebral palsy and was severely handicapped. I was advised to put him in an institution. I had seen enough babies snatched from their mothers' arms that I could not willingly part with my own son. This fragile child had captured my heart, and I knew I had to care for him myself, no matter how difficult it might be.

When my husband was shipped out to Greenland for six months, I was left alone to care for an infant who had frequent seizures and seemed to be in pain much of the time. And yet I was relieved to not have to worry about our stressful marriage. On many a discouraging day, memories of Martin's advice from long-ago kept me going: "Just take one day at a time, Cato." In spite of his problems, Johnny filled my heart with a love that was deeper and more nurturing than I had ever known.

When my husband returned, each day with him seemed more difficult than the last. When Johnny was nineteen months old, I realized that caring for him was beyond me. Several times each day I tried to feed him milk with an eyedropper and he couldn't even take that. A few days after I tearfully placed him in a special home, I received a telephone call in the middle of the night telling me that a powerful convulsion had taken Johnny's life. Johnny's spirit was free, but mine was tormented by an inconsolable grief. I had no one to share my sorrow with, not even my husband. How I missed my beloved little boy.

My second son, Gary, was three months old when Johnny passed away. He was a robust, healthy baby, a son my husband could be proud of. At eight months of age, however, he, too, began having seizures. The same doctor who had assured me of excellent chances for a healthy second baby informed me sadly that Gary had a milder case of the same condition Johnny had. Doomed by the dark shadows of discord and genetic destiny, our marriage ended. I moved to Southern California to raise Gary alone.

Gary was much stronger than Johnny, and I took delight in watching him grow. When he was two, I cut off the toes of some old sneakers that were too small for him and bolted them onto the pedals of a second-hand tricycle. A neighbor welded a backrest onto the seat so Gary could sit up. I fastened a belt around his belly and happily pushed him around the neighborhood. His grin and his shining eyes told me wordlessly that he loved it, too.

I had found a kindhearted and patient Hispanic woman to care for Gary while I worked in a large hospital. It was while I was at this hospital that one of the nurses showed me a catalog where you could trade coupons from cigarette packages for merchandise. Gary was getting too big to carry and for "only" 10,000 coupons, I could get him a wheelchair. So we asked everyone we knew who smoked, but still the stack of coupons grew extremely slowly. When I found out that Mr. Walter Knott, the founder of Knott's Berry Farms was a patient in our hospital, I had an idea. Greet would have thought of it first if she had been here. I gathered my courage and asked Mr. Knott if his groundskeepers could save all the cigarette wrappers they found when they cleaned up at night. I told him of Gary's cerebral palsy and showed him the catalog. He listened sympathetically and agreed to talk to his workers as soon as he was better.

The next day, as I fixed dinner for Gary, a knock came at the door. The driver of a truck with a Knott's Berry Farm emblem on it asked me, "Are you the lady with the kid who needed the wheelchair?"

How could they be bringing me coupons already, I wondered. Where would I put them all? I followed him out to the street and in the back of the truck sat a shiny new child's wheelchair. "Mr. Knott wanted you to have this," the man said. As he lifted the chair on to the grass, I touched the gleaming chrome and could only weep. I was so overcome with joy that I cried late into the night and many nights after. I couldn't believe such generosity from a man I had known only a few hours. Of course, one of our first outings with the treasured wheelchair was to Knott's Berry Farm. I took Gary to shake hands with Mr. Walter Knott to thank him personally.

Soon I met a man who was also divorced. He treated me very well— until we were married. His drinking problem quickly became evident, and like Pa's, his alcohol made him violent and I was his target. I was back in the life I thought I had left in Holland. My husband told me that if we put Gary into a home for handicapped children, the drinking would stop. Sending Gary away was the hardest thing he could have asked me to do, but the tension and confusion in our home was not good for my son. With a sorrowful heart, I had Gary admitted to a special home.

Ten-year-old Gary was very upset with our separation which may have been the cause of even more frequent seizures. And, as I should have known, my husband's promise was forgotten.

On April 25, 1968, my daughter Louisa was born. She was beautifully healthy, all eight pounds and nine ounces of her. Still, I was nervous about bringing a baby into the kind of home I had hated so.

After my two frail boys, I watched Louisa's rapid progress joyfully. Before I knew it, she was walking. I took her often to visit Gary so they could be brother and sister to each other. After awhile I was asked not to come so often because Gary got hysterical every time we had to leave. If only I could have explained things to Gary in a way he could understand. But then, even I couldn't understand why we had to be apart.

When Louisa was about two, my husband beat me brutally and left in a rage to go see a movie. I remember lying on the couch, throbbing with pain, desperately wondering how I could escape. The phone rang. A doctor's voice told me Gary had suffered a convulsion and was not expected to live. Deep in my heart, I knew Gary was already dead. I bundled up Louisa and put her in the car. Blinded by tears, I ran over a boulder and tore a hole in the gas tank. I hitchhiked the rest of the way with Louisa in my arms. As soon as I arrived I learned that my suspicions were right. My dear Gary had died without a mother's good-bye.

My husband refused to be involved in Gary's funeral in any way. Gary's body lay in a mortuary for nine days before a church offered money to help me buy a little white casket to bury him in. I went about my household duties in a daze. Louisa was my only comfort.

When I could think clearly again, I had divorce papers served on my husband. How would I know it would provoke the worst beating of my life? I slept with Louisa in my bed that night, a large knife under my pillow. Early the next morning, we packed up all our belongings and our german shepherd, Lady, and began the long drive to Canada. Somewhere in the midwest, Lady died of old age, and we stopped just long enough to bury her by the side of the road.

My adopted family, "Grandma" and "Grandpa" Cox, and "Aunt" Marion greeted two weary, lonely travelers with open arms. They helped us find an apartment, and I found work as a taxi driver. My husband wrote letters filled with apologies and glittering promises. He wanted us back. Before writing to tell him he could visit us, I conferred with the Coxes, who warned me to be very careful not to become trapped in the same abuse. He arrived in Canada as a changed man, loving, repentant, showering Louisa and me with care. He was not drinking. When he begged me to come back to California, I naively consented.

For the first few months, he was everything I had hoped he would be. So I was shocked when he came home drunk one night. From that time on, our relationship deteriorated again into one of bitter violence. Even after I moved into an apartment of my own, I was afraid for Louisa's safety. We moved back to Canada, this time hoping to stay.

After several happy years, the last step of our journey back to the United States began with severe pains in Louisa's legs. Her doctors said she needed to get away from the harsh, wet winters of Canada and to a drier climate. With a little research, we chose Utah as our destination.

Even this last trip couldn't go smoothly. Our old clunker broke down right on the border and had to be pushed across into the U.S. by the inspectors. Eleven days after leaving home, we arrived in Utah, glad to stay in one place.

Louisa's growth into a bright-eyed and lively child was a daily miracle in my life. I built her a wooden dollhouse in memory of my Uncle Cor. Her blue eyes shone with excitement when I unveiled it. We deco-

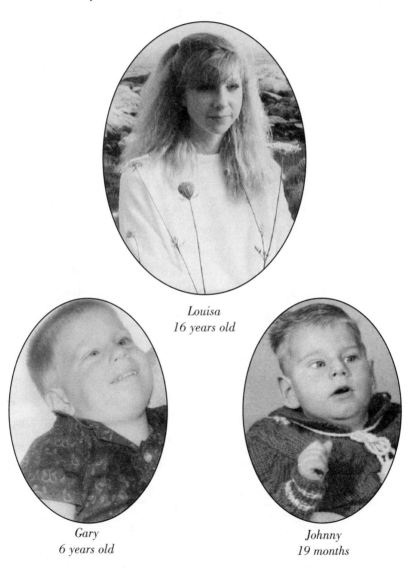

Louisa
16 years old

Gary
6 years old

Johnny
19 months

rated it together and filled it with furniture made out of wood scraps.

Louisa's trusting eyes reminded me of how different her world was from mine. I watched her hands cradle her dolls, I listened to her lullabies, and I grieved for my stolen childhood. It was hard to tuck her into bed each night without flashbacks of my nights on the roof. When I felt my patience wear thin and wanted to rage at her, I remembered the terror Pa struck in my soul. When I took Louisa shopping and she twirled in front of me in a pretty dress, I wondered what it would have been like to have a mother take delight in caring for me. I couldn't remember ever being a little girl. I wanted to fill Louisa with trust and hope and happiness, the rights of every child, but I didn't know if I knew how. I wanted her to see the goodness in a world that had almost destroyed me. I struggled against my memories during the days and against the fiery nightmares that visited me in sleep. As I marked the milestones of her growth, I tried to forget the thousands of children whose lives had ended too soon and of the millions whose innocence was seared by the fires of hatred.

When Louisa was six and we were still living in Canada, I felt a tug at my heart pulling me back to Holland. I had told her very little about my early years and nothing about the camp. I needed to take my daughter to my homeland, for her sake and mine. Saving the money was no easy task, but I began putting away a small portion of my nurse's salary each week until we had enough for our plane tickets.

I suppose we looked like any Dutch mother and daughter as we stood on the bridge near Anne Frank's home and wandered through downtown streets, peeking through the windows of the shops. She held my hand as we walked the path I followed to find refuge in Oma's house. Her eyes were filled with wonder, mine with visions of soldiers and destruction. Ma and Pa seemed like two ordinary grandparents to her. I saw the damage years of drinking had done to Pa and to their marriage. The house was unchanged.

I tried to see Amsterdam as Louisa saw it, a place of charm and warmth and beauty. As we explored, I began to tell her about growing up between the raindrops. I told her of Sonja's faltering steps across the street, of Greet's talent for mischief, and about a man named Mr. Speets, whose words had quietly soothed my troubled heart.

Derk and Piet and their wives seemed distant and uninterested in our lives. Even more bent with age, Uncle Cor invited us to stay in his small basement apartment.

Day after day, I let my memories, good and bad, wash across me like a spring cloudburst. It was as if the Woodpecker, Henny and Jenny, and my folks were walking behind us, chattering at me, reminding me of scenes I had fought for years to forget. I was only two years older than Louisa when I had tried to grab the knife away from Pa. It was difficult for me to believe I had been so small when faced with such peril. Slowly the realization began growing in me that perhaps I had not been able to forget because I was not supposed to. Had it been those memories that gave me strength to love Louisa when I didn't think I could? I began to feel the frightened child in me thank me for keeping her memory alive, for it was she who helped me see in Louisa an innocence I could not let myself destroy. I began to understand that my profound love for my own babies had been born long ago when I stood helplessly before a fire and watched the most delicate of children burn to death before they had tasted life. From the flames of death had come my fierce love of life. Could there be entangled in those memories a strand of hope I could offer someone else?

Martin's memory walked beside me in Amsterdam, too. He stood taller and more heroic than ever. I knew that I could only keep my solemn promise to him by remembering, not forgetting.

Louisa and I came home and then moved to America, and I began to remember and to write. Year after year I have written. I now offer to you and to Martin my promise fulfilled.

EPILOGUE

My life today contains the same mixture of joy and frustration as yours. Louisa, a strong and vivacious young woman, recently graduated from college. I am married to Antonio, a wonderful man from South America. We are not rich, but we are happy together. There is peace in our home. Because of problems with my back, I have had to give up one of my great loves, nursing. I still grieve over that.

Now, I drive a school bus filled with children I worry about. I worry about what happens to them after I drop them off at school. Are they treated with respect no matter how they are dressed, what color their skin is, or what neighborhood they come from? As a schoolgirl I acted tough, as though I didn't care what people thought of my folks, but I wasn't as tough as I tried to appear. It hurts to feel ashamed of where you come from. I wonder if there is a Mr. Speets at school who will take a moment out of a demanding day to look deeply into the eyes of the troubled ones who step from my bus and who will try to understand the burdens their young hearts carry? Without Mr. Speets, my life would have been far different. I could easily have become a perpetrator of cruelty myself.

I worry about the homes the children go back to each afternoon. Will they find peace there? Will they find adults who have time for them, who will listen to their hopes and heartaches so they won't have to search for friendship on the streets? I wonder if a child sees much difference between a parent who is too drunk to care and one who is too busy to care. Are my school-bus friends addicted to video games of such gore and blood that they think violence is a joke? I worry about how they will find their way in the world we have created for them.

I see myself in the faces of these children. Some have been beaten as I was. Some have been so bruised by ridicule, they no longer trust. Some have been so hardened by tough talk and anger, they are ready to destroy. One small boy cannot get on the bus each morning without climbing onto my lap for a hug. What a simple way for me to show him he is welcome in my life. Any kind adults can represent safety to the children around them. You can be the adult who speaks gently and satisfies their hunger for praise, the one who shares with them and forgives their blunders. You can be the adult whose smile tells a child there is kindness in the world.

I tell my story to hundreds of young people every year. It has taken many years to be able to sincerely say I don't feel hate for any group or individual, not even today's skinheads and hate-mongers. What I do feel is great disappointment and sorrow for those who are so far along the path of hatred. And I have to admit I feel deep anger. I don't claim to be a saint.

The Hitler Youth were nothing more than a gang. I have talked to many gang members. Fighting seems to be their life blood. When I look into their faces, I see callousness staring back at me. I see faces filled with hatred. The expressions on their young faces resurrect my buried memories of the faces of the Nazi guards, dead to human feeling. I tell them that just because they're in the gutter now doesn't mean they have to stay there. Hating someone else will never solve our problems. It will only help us escape them for awhile, until it is too late to solve them.

Sometimes just behind the callousness is a silent cry for another chance. If you want a better life, there are people who can help—a Mr. Speets, a Marion Cox, a Walter Knott, perhaps even a Martin. But you have to look for them. You may have to open the door and walk into the room where that teacher is sitting and ask for help. Or apply for a job, or look through the faces of the crowd for a true friend.

In Nordhausen, I learned the meaning of the word *trapped*. I hear people complain of being trapped in a job, a marriage, a group of friends, a lifestyle, or by an addiction. I don't believe it. Until you have someone three times your size standing over you with a whip, a killer dog, and a gun, you are not trapped. You may have to go hungry, or start over in a new place, or admit to a friend that you can't make it alone. Or you may have to tap inner resources you never knew you had in order to change your life. But don't use the excuse of being trapped with me.

Everyone can find a reason, an excuse, to hate. Every one of us has been hurt or cheated by someone. Anyone can find an excuse to hate men, kids, a neighbor, the government, ethnic groups, police officers, poor people, rich people. Excuses are easy to find, to believe, to cling to as if they justify any behavior we choose. But how do these excuses stand up against Martin's or Rosie's. I have profound respect for those who have every reason to hate and choose not to.

Fifty years ago, millions of people used loyalty to a cause or country as an excuse to hate. Thousands of good people perished at the hands of some of my own Dutch countrymen who sided with Hitler. But I am not responsible for those deaths because I am Dutch any more than someone who was born German shares the blame for what Hitler did to the human race. We must stop hating people for wrongs committed before they were born or by others of their nationality or color.

I have hated. I hated the merciless guards of Nordhausen. I hated the murdering Nazis who beat and killed the innocent and the weak. I hated Henny and Jenny for betraying me. I lived on that hate in Nordhausen, and I carried it back to Holland as late as 1973, when I still hoped to run into one of the twins. Today I do not feel hate toward Henny and Jenny, only toward ideologies that preach violence and intolerance and cruelty. My hate for my tormentors has softened into sorrow for what they were capable of doing to babies and children and innocent adults.

Because I know what violence feels like—how it looks, how it hurts, how it kills—I feel we need to take the violence off television. We need to take the profit out of violence. If television executives were forced to spend even twenty-four hours in a concentration camp, perhaps they would learn that violence is not a game. If they experienced the reality of torture at the hands of guards who were indifferent to human suffering, they would know that violence is not entertainment. Do those who make their fortunes by poisoning the minds of our children understand that their own children must live in the society being polluted? Why do they want a generation that considers violence a routine part of life?

We wondered what the Nazi guards told their families about the shimmering jewels they took home. Today I wonder what those who profit from turning violence into an industry tell their families. What would they say if their children greeted them with, "Hi, Daddy, hi, Mommy. How many murders did you parade before my friends today?"

Many citizens of the village of Nordhausen as well as millions of Europeans were blind to what was happening in Germany. Will we allow ourselves to be blind to the effects of glamorized violence in our society? Are we blind to many of today's victims—children who need foster homes, runaways, the poor, victims of age or sex or racial discrimination, or those endowed with below average intellectual ability?

It is impossible to be truly thankful and cruel at the same time. Americans suffer from a severe appreciation deficiency, fed by materialism and acquisitiveness. The same materialism that makes us callous toward others robs us of simple joys. What goes unacknowledged in our lives every day? Must the simple pleasures of life be taken from us before we will feel grateful for fresh air, a pillow, a friend who is still alive in the morning, a bite of fresh bread, a sip of clean water, a family untouched by hate, a mother who is glad we were born, freedom from tyranny, a country at peace, soap, the strength to run, the opportunity to love, a tomorrow we aren't afraid to wake up to?

I can still feel the sting of the hands of the Nazis who beat me, the burning antiseptic baths on arrival at the concentration camp. I can still feel the searing humiliation of trying to shield my naked body from the stares of strangers. Pieces of shrapnel are still in my leg. The Nazis' absolute cruelty grew out of their belief that they were superior human beings and that there existed inferior human beings who were not worthy to live.

There are tyrants as insanely evil as Hitler walking among us today. We must never believe that we can watch cruelty from a distance and not be touched because the hatred is not directed at us. Hatred is a poison of such strength it is like an acid that eats through anything that tries to contain it. I was not a Jew, an enemy of the state, or even an adult. That's the way hatred works—indiscriminately. That's the way it always is. Base your life on callousness toward a group of people, and one day you turn around, and your mother or your little sister or best friend has been destroyed by the hate you thought was directed at someone else. Or you find that your own life has been destroyed. And it all starts with the belief that you are above another human being.

Slowly, very slowly, I have made peace with my grandmother's God—actually more of a truce than a permanent peace. I feel a strong belief in a supreme power, a source of goodness and of the earth's beauty. I'm afraid I don't talk to him very much. I still have too many questions for him. I am unwilling to believe in any doctrine that labels someone else's feelings about God as wrong. Although I have great admiration for my friends of many denominations, I could not risk aligning myself with any group which may create more division than unity among people. Oma's God understands why.

I am as stubborn as I ever was. I am still too stubborn to let anyone make my decisions for me. I am stubborn enough to say what needs to be said, to look gang members in the face and tell them what cowards they are and what an ugly world they are creating for their brothers and sisters. I guess you could say I'm just too stubborn to keep my mouth shut. And too stubborn not to keep a promise made so long ago to Martin that the world will not forget the ashes of our friends.